INDIANS

BLACK HAWK, *Cleven*
CHIEF JOSEPH, *Burt*
OSCEOLA, *Clark*
POCAHONTAS, *Seymour*
PONTIAC, *Peckham*
SACAGAWEA, *Seymour*
SEQUOYAH, *Snow*
SITTING BULL, *Stevenson*
SQUANTO, *Stevenson*
TECUMSEH, *Stevenson*

NAVAL HEROES

DAVID FARRAGUT, *Long*
GEORGE DEWEY, *Long*
JOHN PAUL JONES, *Snow*
MATTHEW CALBRAITH PERRY, *Scharbach*
OLIVER HAZARD PERRY, *Long*
RAPHAEL SEMMES, *Snow*
STEPHEN DECATUR, *Smith*

NOTED WIVES and MOTHERS

ABIGAIL ADAMS, *Wagoner*
DOLLY MADISON, *Monsell*
ELEANOR ROOSEVELT, *Weil*
JESSIE FREMONT, *Wagoner*
MARTHA WASHINGTON, *Wagoner*
MARY TODD LINCOLN, *Wilkie*
NANCY HANKS, *Stevenson*
RACHEL JACKSON, *Govan*

SCIENTISTS and INVENTORS

ABNER DOUBLEDAY, *Dunham*
ALBERT EINSTEIN, *Hammontree*
ALECK BELL, *Widdemer*
CYRUS McCORMICK, *Dobler*
ELI WHITNEY, *Snow*
ELIAS HOWE, *Corcoran*
ELIZABETH BLACKWELL, *Henry*
GAIL BORDEN, *Paradis*
GEORGE CARVER, *Stevenson*
GEORGE EASTMAN, *Henry*
GEORGE PULLMAN, *Myers*
GEORGE WESTINGHOUSE, *Dunham*
GLENN L. MARTIN, *Harley*
HENRY FORD, *Aird and Ruddiman*
JEAN FELIX PICCARD, *de Grummond and Delaune*
JOHN AUDUBON, *Mason*
JOHN BURROUGHS, *Frisbee*
JOHN DEERE, *Bare*
JOHN FITCH, *Stevenson*
LEE DEFOREST, *Dobler*
LUTHER BURBANK, *Burt*
MARIA MITCHELL, *Melin*
ROBERT FULTON, *Henry*
ROBERT GODDARD, *Moore*
SAMUEL MORSE, *Snow*

WILL AND CHARLIE MAYO, *Hammontree*

SOCIAL and CIVIC LEADERS

BETSY ROSS, *Weil*
BOOKER T. WASHINGTON, *Stevenson*
CLARA BARTON, *Stevenson*
DAN BEARD, *Mason*
DOROTHEA DIX, *Melin*
FRANCES WILLARD, *Mason*
HELEN KELLER, *Wilkie*
J. STERLING MORTON, *Moore*
JANE ADDAMS, *Wagoner*
JOHN PETER ZENGER, *Long*
JULIA WARD HOWE, *Wagoner*
JULIETTE LOW, *Higgins*
LILIUOKALANI, *Newman*
LUCRETIA MOTT, *Burnett*
MARTIN LUTHER KING, JR., *Millender*
MOLLY PITCHER, *Stevenson*
OLIVER WENDELL HOLMES, JR., *Dunham*
ROBERT TODD LINCOLN, *Anderson*
SUSAN ANTHONY, *Monsell*

SOLDIERS

ALVIN C. YORK, *Weddle*
ANTHONY WAYNE, *Stevenson*
BEDFORD FORREST, *Parks*
DAN MORGAN, *Bryant*
DOUGLAS MacARTHUR, *Long*
ETHAN ALLEN, *Winders*
FRANCIS MARION, *Steele*
GEORGE CUSTER, *Stevenson*
ISRAEL PUTNAM, *Stevenson*
JEB STUART, *Winders*
NATHANAEL GREENE, *Peckham*
ROBERT E. LEE, *Monsell*
SAM HOUSTON, *Stevenson*
TOM JACKSON, *Monsell*
U. S. GRANT, *Stevenson*
WILLIAM HENRY HARRISON, *Peckham*
ZACK TAYLOR, *Wilkie*

STATESMEN

ABE LINCOLN, *Stevenson*
ADLAI STEVENSON, *Ward*
ANDY JACKSON, *Stevenson*
DAN WEBSTER, *Smith*
FRANKLIN ROOSEVELT, *Weil*
HENRY CLAY, *Monsell*
HERBERT HOOVER, *Comfort*
JAMES MONROE, *Widdemer*
JEFF DAVIS, *de Grummond and Delaune*
JOHN F. KENNEDY, *Frisbee*
JOHN MARSHALL, *Monsell*
TEDDY ROOSEVELT, *Parks*
WOODROW WILSON, *Monsell*

John
Philip Sousa

Marching Boy

Illustrated by Katherine Sampson

John
Philip Sousa

Marching Boy

By Ann Weil

the NEW *Bobbs-Merrill* COMPANY, INC.

® AN ASSOCIATE OF HOWARD W. SAMS & CO., INC.

Publishers • INDIANAPOLIS • NEW YORK

92
Sou

LIBRARY OF CONGRESS CATALOG CARD NUMBER: 59-12856

PRINTED IN THE UNITED STATES OF AMERICA

To Steven and David

The author is indebted to Helen Sousa Abert
for permission to adapt certain incidents and to use
brief quotations from Marching Along:
Recollections of Men, Women, and Music,
by John Philip Sousa.

Illustrations

PAGE

Full pages

"Don't we look funny?" said Philip.   32

Philip sounded out the rhythm perfectly.   51

The bow broke in two pieces.   59

"Look at me. I'm marching."   101

There stood Philip in the baggy shirt.   117

The children watched the parade.   137

"I need musicians for my band."   145

"How do you fold a coat?"   160

General Zeilin welcomed Philip.   167

Mr. Corcoran asked many questions.   181

Numerous smaller illustrations

Contents

	PAGE		PAGE
The Singing Lesson	11	Philip Plays Happy Music	121
The Lost Spectacles	26	The Circus Parade	130
The Silent One	40	Philip Meets a Band Leader	140
Philip Changes His Mind	56	The Carpetbag	153
The Bakery Shop	65	The Sunday Suit	163
Philip and the President	77	The Big Opportunity	175
Marching in the Parade	95	The March King	184
The Borrowed Shirt	106		

Books by Ann Weil

BETSY ROSS: GIRL OF OLD PHILADELPHIA
FRANKLIN ROOSEVELT: BOY OF THE FOUR FREEDOMS
JOHN PHILIP SOUSA: MARCHING BOY
JOHN QUINCY ADAMS: BOY PATRIOT

John
Philip Sousa

Marching Boy

The Singing Lesson

"PHILIP!" said Mr. Sousa to his five-year-old son. "John Philip!"

"Yes, Papa," replied Philip.

"There's someone at the door," said Mr. Sousa. "Please see who it is."

Philip knew, before he opened the door, who would be on the other side. Several times a week, after supper, Mr. and Mrs. Esputa came for a visit. Mr. Esputa, an old Spanish gentleman, was one of Mr. Sousa's best friends.

"Good evening. Good evening," said Mr. Esputa, as Philip opened the door. He always greeted Philip as if he were a grown man.

"Good evening," said Philip, shaking hands with both Mr. and Mrs. Esputa.

A few minutes later Mr. Sousa and Mr. Esputa were sitting beside the large library table, talking together. Mrs. Esputa and Mrs. Sousa were in their usual corner beside the stove.

Philip looked around the room. He wished he had someone to play with him. His older sister, Tinnie, was upstairs reading. His younger brothers, George and Tony, were already in bed. They were too little to play with, anyhow.

Philip found a ball and began to bounce it. "Papa, may I go outside?" he asked.

"Now? Why, it's pitch-dark," said Mr. Sousa. "It's too late to play outside."

Philip sat down on the floor and rolled the ball across the room. Then he jumped up, picked up the ball, sat down, and rolled it again.

Soon Philip discovered that if he rolled the ball hard enough to hit the wall, it would bounce back to him. This was more fun than having to go after the ball each time he rolled it.

Philip rolled the ball harder and harder, and faster and faster. The harder and faster he rolled it, the more noise it made.

"Philip!" Mr. Sousa looked down at his son. "You are making too much noise. Don't roll the ball so hard. Mr. Esputa and I can't hear what we're saying to each other."

"Philip is a very lively boy," said Mr. Esputa. "He also has a mind of his own."

"Yes, if he really wants something," said Mr. Sousa, "he will get it, never fear!"

For a while Philip really tried to play quietly with the ball. It wasn't easy to do. Unless he made the ball hit the wall rather hard, it wouldn't come all the way back to him.

Soon Philip found that he could keep time with the ball. If he rolled it evenly, it sounded like a drum when it hit the wall.

Then he forgot all about his father and Mr. Esputa. Now he was having fun! He imagined that he was beating a drum. Back and forth went the ball. Louder and louder grew the thumps.

"Philip!" Mr. Sousa looked down again. "Mr. Esputa and I are shouting, and still we can't hear each other."

"But there's nothing to do," said Philip, jumping up from the floor. "Tinnie won't play with me. And you won't let me go outside. There's nothing to do."

"Nothing to do? Nothing to do?" Mr. Esputa waved his hands as he spoke. "A big boy like you—five years old—and nothing to do! There is everything to do. And there is so much to learn. You should not waste your time rolling a ball back and forth. Look, I will teach you how to sing. How would you like that?

"Yes," Mr. Esputa went on. "Each time I come I'll give you a lesson. What do you say?"

14

Philip looked at his father, and Mr. Sousa looked at Mr. Esputa.

"Well—" Mr. Sousa pulled his beard— "I don't know. I want Philip to study music, but I think he is a little young to start."

"Young?" Mr. Esputa looked surprised. "No one is ever too young to study music. Look at some of the great composers. They started when they were two or three years old."

Mr. Esputa paused. He thought that Mr. Sousa was changing his mind. "I remember," he went on, "I started my son, John, when he was four. Now he is a good musician."

Mr. Esputa looked over his spectacles at Philip. "What do you think, my boy?"

"I'm old enough to learn," replied Philip proudly. "I have learned a lot of things already. I know that I live in Washington, D.C., and that it's the capital of our country. I know that I was born on November 6, 1854. I know the names of the days of the week and the months of the year. I know that this is 1859. I know——"

"See!" Mr. Esputa looked at Mr. Sousa. "This boy, he is bright." He looked at Philip again. "Five years old, eh? Why, you certainly are old enough to start. Perhaps too old!"

"Too old?" said Mr. Sousa. "Too old? Ridiculous! Nonsense! What a thing to say! But perhaps, after all, Philip is not too young. If he wants to study with you, it is all right with me."

Philip was delighted. He threw his arms around his mother and hugged her.

"Oh, Mamma!" he cried. "Did you hear? I'm going to take singing lessons!"

Mrs. Sousa smoothed Philip's hair. "That's fine, Philip," she said. She knew that Philip had been begging to learn to play a trombone. So she added, "If you learn to sing well, maybe you can learn to play a trombone later."

Now that Mr. Sousa had given his consent, he

16

was pleased, too. He never had heard his friend sing, but he was sure that Mr. Esputa knew a great deal about music. Philip was lucky to have such a wonderful music teacher.

Mr. Esputa was more pleased than anyone else. For years he had played with a good orchestra. Now he was too old for that, but he still loved music.

Mr. Esputa put his spectacles on the end of his nose. He rubbed his hands together. He cleared his throat. "Now!" He looked at Philip proudly and smiled. "Let us begin. I will sing the first note of the scale. Then you repeat it after me, exactly as I sing it."

Mr. Esputa took a deep breath. Then he tried to sing *do*, but only a squeaky sound came out.

Philip had a fine ear for tone. He was very eager to imitate Mr. Esputa perfectly. *"Do,"* he squeaked back, making exactly the same sound that Mr. Esputa had made.

17

"No! No! No!" Mr. Esputa waved his hands in the air. "That is not *do*. You sound like a crow. Now listen carefully."

When Mr. Esputa was calm, he squeaked. When he was excited, he squawked. This time he was excited. "*Do*," he squawked.

"*Do*," squawked Philip.

"No! No! No! Now you sound like a duck."

The lesson went on and on. Finally both Mr. Esputa and Philip were too tired to speak.

"Well," said Mr. Sousa after Mr. and Mrs. Esputa had left for home. "Do you still want to take singing lessons, Philip?"

Philip thought of Mr. Esputa's terrible voice and his excited manner. Then he thought about learning to play a trombone.

"Papa?"

"Yes, Philip."

"I'd rather take trombone lessons from you. I want to play in the Marine Band with you. I want to wear a uniform just like yours."

Mr. Sousa walked over to some shelves in the corner of the living room. He picked up a long, black case and took out his trombone.

"Here, Philip," he said. "Let's see whether you can play it."

Philip took the trombone in his hands. It was big! It was long! And it was heavy!

At last Philip managed to hold the trombone almost straight out. He put his lips to the mouth-

19

piece. He took a deep breath. Then he blew with all his might.

Philip looked at the trombone and then at his father. What was wrong? Where was the music? Why didn't the trombone play?

Mr. Sousa sat down on a chair and put his arm around Philip's shoulders. "You see, Philip," he said, "a trombone is big, and you must be big before you can play it. But singing—" he smiled at the eager boy— "singing comes in all sizes. There are songs for five-year-olds, for ten-year-olds, and for grownups.

"I know Mr. Esputa doesn't have a good voice," Mr. Sousa went on, "but he knows music well. He can teach you a lot about music and then—" Mr. Sousa took Philip's arm and measured it against the trombine— "when your arms are ready for trombone lessons, you'll be ready, too. Ready for trombone lessons and——"

Mr. Sousa didn't finish the sentence. He stood

20

up and put his trombone away. Then he walked across the room to a big chest. The chest had a high, rounded lid. It had a black lock on the front and leather handles on the sides.

Philip knew that his father had brought the old chest from Spain. He knew, too, that his mother took special care of it. Every day she dusted it carefully with a soft cloth.

The chest had pictures of Spanish people on the sides. Philip thought they looked as if they were marching—round and round. Sometimes he marched back and forth in front of the chest, pretending to lead the painted people.

Now as Philip looked at the chest, all the people on the sides seemed to be standing still. They seemed to be waiting, as Philip was, to see what Mr. Sousa was going to do.

Mr. Sousa put the key in the lock. The lock squeaked when he turned the key. The hinges squawked when he lifted the heavy lid.

Mr. Sousa looked at Philip and laughed. "You know," he said, "I think this old chest has been taking singing lessons from Mr. Esputa. But," he added quickly, "like Mr. Esputa, it also has something good to give us."

Philip looked first at the chest and then at his father. He always had thought that the chest was empty. Now he could see that it wasn't.

Mr. Sousa reached into the chest and brought out a black case. Then, putting it on the table, he opened it very carefully.

"A violin!" Philip climbed up on a chair so that he could see better. "Oh, Papa! It's beautiful! Where did you get it?"

Mr. Sousa lifted the violin out of its case. "It belonged to my father," he said. "He could play beautiful music on it. Many times when I was a boy about your size, I begged him to let me play it. But he never would let me. He would not even let me touch it.

"Whenever I hear a violin, I think of the old days in Spain. We sat on the floor, as quiet as mice, while Papa played. Ah, yes, in Spain everyone loved music. In Mamma's country, Bavaria, everyone loved music, too."

Mr. Sousa handed the violin to Philip. "Some day when you are old enough to play this violin, it shall be yours."

"Oh, Papa!" Philip was so excited that he didn't know what to say. "Mine? Really mine? Really and truly mine?"

Mr. Sousa laughed. "Really and truly yours," he said. "I never learned to play it, but some day I hope that you will."

"Oh, I will, Papa. I will," cried Philip, running his fingers over the smooth reddish-brown wood. He was sure that this was the most beautiful violin in all the world.

The clock on the mantel began to strike. "Bedtime," said Mr. Sousa. "Five-year-old musicians need a lot of sleep."

"Good night, Papa." Philip started toward the stairs. Then he stopped. "Look, Papa," he said, pointing toward the stairway. "The steps go up like the notes on a scale."

Mr. Sousa laughed. "That's right, Philip," he said. "They're notes that your feet can sing. Now PRESTO AND PIANISSIMO."

Philip looked at his father. "What do those words mean?" he asked.

"PRESTO means very fast," Mr. Sousa explained. "And PIANISSIMO means very softly. Don't you think that's a good way for your feet to sing on their way to bed?"

Philip ran up the stairs as quickly and quietly as he could. Then, leaning over the banister, he called down, "Papa!"

"Yes, Philip?"

"Did my feet sing all right?"

Mr. Sousa nodded. "Fine," he called back. "They were very good pupils. I'm sure Mr. Esputa would be proud of them."

The Lost
Spectacles

THE SINGING LESSONS went on and on. In spite of Mr. Esputa's terrible voice, Philip loved to sing. He liked lively, jolly songs best of all.

Mr. Esputa had Philip spend hours practicing scales. He always started his singing lessons in the same way.

"Now, we'll see what you have learned. Stand straight, shoulders back. One, two, three, sing! *Do, re, mi, fa, sol, la, ti, do.*"

Mr. Esputa had Philip go over the scales time and time again. Sometimes he would stop him right in the middle of the scales. "Head up!" or "Take a deep breath," he would call out to him.

Then, near the end of the lesson, he would let Philip sing a real song.

Philip complained a few times to his father about Mr. Esputa.

Mr. Sousa always had the same answer when Philip complained. "Only stupid people get angry when they are corrected, my son. A real musician learns to take criticism, and to do something about it. You are a real musician. Listen to Mr. Esputa."

Sometimes Philip sang little songs for Tinnie and George. Tinnie liked to sing along with Philip. Little George had trouble learning the words, but he sang with Philip anyhow.

Some evenings after Mr. and Mrs. Esputa had gone home, Philip would say, "Papa, let me look at my violin."

At this Mr. Sousa would put down his book and take the violin from the chest.

Philip would take the violin gently in his

hands and run his fingers over the smooth wood. Then, when it was time to put the violin away, he would say, "Papa, when will I be big enough to play my violin?"

"H-m-m-m," Mr. Sousa would pretend to measure Philip with his eyes. "Well," he would say, "if you keep on eating Mamma's good cooking, it shouldn't be very long."

Sometimes Philip wasn't very happy about taking his lesson. One evening when Mr. Esputa came, he looked down at Philip and said, "Ah, my boy! You are ready, yes?"

Philip nodded his head, but he really wasn't ready. He didn't want to take his lesson. He didn't want to hear Mr. Esputa's squeaky voice. He didn't want to practice scales.

·Mr. Esputa reached into his pocket for his spectacles. "Ay, my spectacles," he cried. "My spectacles! They're gone. They're not in my coat. Where can they be?"

He became very excited. He looked through all the pockets in his clothes.

"Mamma!" He called to his wife. "Mamma! I can't find my spectacles."

Mrs. Esputa scarcely lifted her eyes from her knitting. "Such a man!" she said to Mrs. Sousa. "He never can find anything.

"Always he is losing his spectacles," she went on. "Then he shouts and screams until he finds them. Usually he finds them on the end of his nose."

Mrs. Esputa called to her husband, "Are they on the end of your nose?"

"The end of my nose! Of course not!" Mr. Esputa's voice rose higher and higher.

"Then look in your pockets, Papa."

"Look in my pockets!" Mr. Esputa put his hands to his head in great disgust. "Listen to the foolish woman. What do you think I have been doing? Standing on my head?"

Everybody, including Philip, looked for the spectacles. At last, even Mrs. Esputa agreed that they might be lost. "I know that you had them on when we left home," she said.

Mr. Esputa nodded his head. He remembered putting them on. "Ay!" he cried. "I must have taken them off again and lost them on the way."

Mr. Sousa opened the closet door and put on his coat. "Philip," he said, "go upstairs and get Tinnie. Then we'll walk back to Mr. Esputa's house to look for his spectacles."

All this made Philip very happy. Looking for spectacles would be much more fun than having a singing lesson. He started up the steps, calling to his sister as he went.

"I brought my spectacles from Spain," said Mr. Esputa mournfully. "I'll never get another pair like them. And without them I am lost."

"Maybe you'll find them," said Mrs. Sousa.

Mr. Esputa's voice boomed. "We'll never find

them," he shouted. "There's no use looking. It's pitch-dark outside. How could we see them?"

Philip stopped at the head of the stairs and waited. What if Mr. Esputa should decide not to look for his glasses? Wouldn't it be too bad to have to take a music lesson, after all?

"Come, now!" said Mr. Sousa to Mr. Esputa. "Don't be upset because you've lost your spectacles. We'll organize a searching party to look for them. And there's a good chance, I think, that we'll find them."

Philip hurried on.

"Tinnie!" he called. "Come downstairs. Mr. Esputa has lost his glasses, and we want you to help look for them."

A few minutes later Mr. Sousa, Mr. Esputa, Tinnie and Philip started out to look for the spectacles. Each of them carried a lighted candle.

Mr. Sousa and Mr. Esputa led the way. Tinnie and Philip followed.

Bending over, they all walked very slowly, holding their candles close to the ground.

Philip looked at Tinnie and began to giggle. "Don't we look funny," he said, "walking along bent over like this?"

Tinnie began to giggle, too. "We look like dwarfs," she said. "Like dwarfs climbing up mountains to look for gold."

"Like marching dwarfs!" said Philip. "Left! Right! Left! Right!" He swung his candle like a baton as he spoke. "Left!"

Philip looked at his candle. "Wait, Tinnie," he called. "My candle has gone out."

"No wonder!" Tinnie looked at him and laughed. "Marching! You're always marching! But even you, John Philip Sousa, can't march with a lighted candle."

Tinnie stopped and let him light his candle from her flame. "Now be good," she whispered. "Don't do any more marching."

Philip laughed. "But walking is easier when you march," he said. "Much easier. Left——"

Tinnie called to Philip again. "No more marching," she ordered.

Philip walked along bent over and tried to hold his candle close to the ground. He kept looking for the spectacles, but imagined all the while that he was marching. "Left! Right! Left! Right!" he whispered to himself. "Left! Right!"

The searchers walked to the end of the block and crossed the street. They walked another block and came to Mr. Esputa's house. Then they walked up some steps onto Mr. Esputa's porch.

"Well, here we are," said Mr. Esputa, "and we haven't found my spectacles. What did I tell you? We'll never find them. Never!"

But Mr. Sousa was more hopeful. "We'll look for them on the way back," he said. "Perhaps we have missed them. They have to be some place."

34

On the way home Philip and Tinnie went on ahead, looking for the spectacles. Mr. Sousa and Mr. Esputa followed along behind.

"Look! We're home already," said Philip. For a moment he forgot all about the spectacles, and cried, "I'll race you to the door."

Tinnie and Philip ran down the path, up the steps and across the porch.

"I won," cried Tinnie. "I——"

But Philip wasn't listening. Out of the corner of his eye he saw something bright and shiny lying on the porch. He walked over and stooped down. There were the spectacles!

"Look!" Philip held the spectacles up for Tinnie to see. "Look what I found."

"Philip, you found them! How wonderful!" Tinnie jumped up and down. "Won't Mr. Esputa be pleased? Let's run and tell him."

They started down the steps, but suddenly Tinnie stopped. "Listen, Philip," she said. "Let's

35

not give them to him now. Let's wait until every-one is inside and surprise him."

Philip nodded. "That's a good idea," he said. "But when——"

"Sh!" Tinnie whispered. "Here come Papa and Mr. Esputa. Put the spectacles in your pocket and don't say anything."

Mrs. Esputa and Mrs. Sousa were waiting in the living room. One look at Mr. Esputa's face told them that he hadn't found his spectacles. They could see that he was very unhappy.

"Well, well," said Mrs. Sousa, trying to be helpful. "Perhaps you'll find your spectacles to-morrow." Then she motioned to Philip and Tin-nie, who were standing near her. "Go into the kitchen and bring in a plate of cookies," she whispered. "Perhaps if we have some cookies, Mr. Esputa will forget all about his spectacles."

Philip and Tinnie ran into the kitchen. Then they closed the door behind them and laughed.

36

"When shall we give Mr. Esputa's spectacles back to him?" asked Tinnie.

"I know," answered Philip. "Let's put them on top of the plate of cookies."

"That's a wonderful idea!" said Tinnie. "You get the plate, and I'll get the cookies."

Together they put the cookies on the plate. Then, when the plate was almost full, Philip took the spectacles out of his pocket and put them on top of the cookies.

"Oh, Philip, this is fun." Tinnie ran to open the kitchen door. "Be sure to pass the cookies to Mr. Esputa first," she whispered.

Philip walked across the room very slowly. Then he stopped in front of Mr. Esputa. "Will you have a cookie?" he asked.

Mr. Esputa looked down at the plate. He couldn't see very well without his spectacles. "What kind are they, Philip?" he asked.

"Chocolate and caramel."

"Chocolate and caramel, eh? Which ones are chocolate?" Mr. Esputa looked closer.

"My spectacles! My dear spectacles!" he exclaimed. "I can hardly believe my eyes, but here they are." He looked at Philip and laughed. "Where did you find them, my boy?"

"On the porch," said Philip.

Mr. Sousa and the others crowded around Philip and Mr. Esputa. They looked at the spectacles as if they never had seen them before.

"Ay!" Mr. Esputa shook his finger at Philip. "Young man," he said, "I knew you had sharp ears. Now I find that you have sharp eyes, too. That's a good combination for a musician."

Philip laughed. No matter what he did, it always seemed to be connected with music—even finding Mr. Esputa's glasses!

"That's strange," said Philip, "because I really want to be a musician. Once I get my violin, I'll practice and practice. Then Papa will be pleased and Mr. Esputa will be pleased. But I'll be pleased most of all."

The Silent One

MR. SOUSA liked to go hunting, and he liked to take Philip with him. Philip wasn't big enough to carry a gun, but it made him feel grown-up to go along and carry the lunch.

One day Mr. Sousa and Philip got up early and went quail hunting. Philip couldn't walk as fast as his father did, and by the middle of the morning he was far behind.

"I'm hungry," Philip decided. He knew that his mother always packed a big lunch. It wouldn't matter if he ate part of it now.

He ate a hard-boiled egg. Strangely, that made him hungrier than ever. He closed the

40

basket and walked on, but he was still hungry. Time and again he reached into the basket and took out one thing and ate it.

Shortly before noon, Philip caught up with his father. "I'm glad to see you," said Mr. Sousa. "I'm ready for some lunch."

Mr. Sousa looked in the basket, but he could hardly believe his eyes. There was nothing in it except one apple! Philip was surprised, too. He hadn't meant to eat so much of the lunch.

Mr. Sousa looked at the little pieces of egg and the crumbs around Philip's mouth. "Here," he said, handing the apple to Philip. "This is for you, but before you eat it—" he pointed to a stream— "you'd better wash your face."

Nothing more was said about the missing lunch, but Philip was worried. Perhaps his father never would ask him to go hunting again. Day after day he waited, but his father didn't say a word about going on a hunting trip.

Then one Friday evening, Philip and George were playing in the living room. Their father was there, too, reading. He looked up from his book and said, "I'm going duck hunting in the morning. Who wants to carry the lunch?"

George was only four, but he tried to do anything that Philip could do. "I do, Papa," he answered at once. "I want to go."

Philip sat up very straight. "I'm the best lunch-carrier in Washington, D.C.," he said, "and I'm really very busy, but——"

"The best lunch-*eater*, you mean," said Mr. Sousa, laughing. "Well, whoever is going with me in the morning must get up at four o'clock."

It was cold and dark at four o'clock the next morning, but Philip didn't mind. He tried to waken George. He shook him by the shoulder, but the little boy only opened one eye.

"It's time to go duck hunting," Philip whispered. "Papa's downstairs already."

George snuggled down in the warm blankets. "Don't bother me," he said sleepily. Then he closed his eyes and went to sleep again.

Philip gave up trying to waken his brother. He picked up a heavy jacket and left the room.

Again Philip felt very grown-up. It was exciting to tiptoe down the stairs when everyone else was asleep. It was even exciting to eat the burned toast, the crisp bacon, and the hard-fried eggs that he and his father cooked.

And it was exciting to walk down the empty streets when the stars were still shining.

On these trips Mr. Sousa usually asked Philip how many ducks he thought they would get. Today he asked something different.

"Philip," said Mr. Sousa, "what do you think you want to be when you grow up?"

"Why, Papa!" Philip was very much surprised. "I thought you knew. I want to be a musician. I'm going to play my violin."

Mr. Sousa smiled. "You've been saying that for a long time, Philip. But are you sure?"

"Yes, I'm sure," answered Philip. "I've always wanted to be a musician. I can't imagine ever being anything else."

Philip and his father walked along in silence for a few minutes. Then Mr. Sousa said, "Mr. Esputa's son, John, came to see me yesterday. He's starting a music school, and would like to have you as a pupil."

44

Mr. Sousa looked down at Philip, but it was still too dark to see his face very clearly.

"Instead of teaching you to read and write words, he'll teach you to read and write music," Mr. Sousa explained. "He'll have all kinds of special classes in music. And he thought that you might want to take lessons on your violin."

"Oh, Papa, may I?" Philip's voice was eager and excited. "May I go to his school? And may I take lessons on my violin?"

"Well—" Mr. Sousa sounded very thoughtful— "if you're going to be a musician, I want you to be a good one. You have a fine ear for music, and you have a good sense of rhythm. Even so, you won't find music easy. You'll have to spend many years just practicing."

"I understand, Papa. But I'll practice very hard. Truly I will."

"You know, of course, that we have very little money," said Mr. Sousa. "With five children to feed and clothe, we have to spend nearly all our money to live. But if you want to go to John Esputa's school—" he put his arm around Philip's shoulders— "we'll manage somehow."

"Oh, Papa!" he cried. "I'll practice and practice every day. You'll see!"

Mr. Sousa squeezed the boy's shoulders. "I believe you, my son," he said. "Now, let's get on with our duck hunting. How many ducks do you think we'll get today?"

"Ten!" said Philip. "Maybe twenty."

Mr. Sousa laughed. "And I say we'll be lucky if we get five."

When Philip and his father returned that afternoon, each of them carried three ducks. Philip didn't say much about the hunting trip. He was more interested in the new music school. He was excited about learning to play his violin.

Philip hurried to tell his best friend about the school. He didn't have far to go, because Edward lived next door. Philip found him in the back yard, batting a baseball.

"Edward," Philip called, "do you know that Mr. John Esputa is starting a music school? Papa and I are going there Monday afternoon."

Edward frowned as he swung his bat. "Yes, I know. He talked with my mother, and I'm going, too." Edward didn't sound very happy.

"That's wonderful, Ed," said Philip. He hadn't noticed that Edward wasn't pleased.

Edward stared in surprise. "I don't want to go," he said. "But my mother wants me to learn to play the alto horn. We'll never have time for baseball, if we take music lessons."

"Oh, yes, we will," laughed Philip.

After school on Monday, Mr. Sousa and Philip went to see John Esputa. When they arrived, many other boys and girls were already there.

"I had no idea that John would have so many pupils," said Mr. Sousa.

When Philip and his father finally reached the office, John Esputa looked up and smiled a little uncertainly. He had not expected so many pupils either. "Quit shoving," he called to the children in a loud voice. "Stand in line there. All right, now. Let's have less noise."

As he talked, he picked up a card and began to fill in the first line. "John Philip Sousa," he wrote. Then he squinted at Philip. "Age?"

"I'm past six," Philip answered quickly.

"He's eager to come to your school, John," said Mr. Sousa. "I hope he'll be a good pupil."

"Well—" John Esputa was so rushed and so excited he scarcely knew what he was saying. "Well," he repeated, "even if he doesn't learn anything, at least he'll be off the streets."

Philip didn't have much to say as he walked home with his father. He wasn't very happy about Mr. Esputa's school, after all. There was something about the teacher that frightened him. His mother and father never shouted as Mr. John Esputa did.

A frown wrinkled Philip's forehead. He had been feeling so grown-up, but now he wasn't sure. He squared his shoulders. No one must ever know that he was afraid.

Suddenly Philip had an idea. He would keep quiet, so the teacher wouldn't notice him. He would do everything he was told to do. He would study hard and practice faithfully. But he wouldn't speak in music school unless he had to. He would be as quiet as he could when he took his lessons. Surely Mr. Esputa wouldn't shout at him then.

Philip and Edward went to music school for an hour every afternoon after regular school. Edward tried to find out why Philip was so silent in music school. But Philip wouldn't admit, even to Edward, that he was afraid of Mr. Esputa.

One of the things John Esputa taught was the

importance of rhythm. Usually he told the class whether a song was written in 3/4 time or 4/4 time or whatever it happened to be. He asked one pupil to sound out the rhythm, after which the group sang the song together.

Mr. Esputa noticed Philip's silence, but he said nothing about it until one day when he passed out some music. "This song is written in 3/4 time," he said. "Will The Silent One sound out the rhythm for us?"

Nobody had called Philip by that name before, but everyone knew whom Mr. Esputa meant. The children laughed.

Philip's cheeks began to burn. He didn't say a word, but he took the music and sounded out the rhythm perfectly.

A buzz of approval ran through the class. The teacher made no comment, but a few of the bolder children took up Mr. Esputa's joke.

"Good for The Silent One!" said one boy.

50

"The Silent One is not always so silent," said one of Philip's friends.

This was only the beginning of the children's good-natured teasing. But no amount of teasing made any difference. Finally John Esputa decided to ignore Philip altogether. Philip didn't care. Now no one shouted at him.

Besides the class lessons in rhythm, there were class lessons in sight reading and harmony, and individual lessons on instruments. Even though Philip was silent, he greatly enjoyed the lessons in harmony. He always knew what chords Mr. Esputa struck on the piano. But he never offered to tell other members of the class.

John Esputa gave individual lessons on instruments after the regular class periods and on Saturdays. Edward took his lesson on Friday, and Philip always waited to walk home with him. While Philip waited, he tried to play with cymbals, a triangle, and even an old alto horn that

52

he found in the classroom. He did very well with all of them.

Every evening Philip practiced and practiced on his violin. At first he practiced to keep Mr. Esputa from shouting at him when he took his lessons. Then, as he became more skillful, he practiced because he loved the music he could make on his violin.

One afternoon toward the end of his third year in John Esputa's school, Philip came home and put his books on the living room table. "Exams! Exams! Exams!" he said. "I have arithmetic and spelling exams tomorrow. We have already had five exams in music school this week."

"I heard about your music examinations, Philip." Mr. Sousa looked up from the paper he was reading. "John Esputa came over to see me today. He told me about them."

Philip nodded. "They were very important

exams," he said. "Mr. Esputa is going to give a medal to the pupil who makes the highest score in each one." Philip stacked his books in a neat pile on the table. "I hope I win one of them."

Mr. Sousa shook his head. "I'm afraid you didn't win one, Philip," he said. "One pupil in the school won all five medals."

"All five? Whee!" Philip gave a low whistle. "Who was it? Did Mr. Esputa say?"

Mr. Sousa picked up his paper and held it in front of his face. "Someone with an odd kind of nickname," he said. "Let's see now, what did John say that the nickname is? Oh, yes. Now I remember. It's The Silent One. That's what it is—The Silent One."

"Papa!" Philip ran across the room and stood beside his father's chair. "Did I? Did I really? Did I win all five medals?"

"I'm afraid so." Mr. Sousa laughed. "And I'm afraid you've caused John trouble."

54

"Trouble?" Philip looked puzzled.

"Well, you see," Mr. Sousa went on, "John knows you made the highest scores on all the exams, and that means you should have all five medals. But, if he gives all the medals to you, he fears the other children will feel discouraged.

"I told him that what you learned was more important than getting medals. But John was very upset. He said he stayed up all night, trying to decide what to do. Finally he decided to give three medals to you, and two to other pupils. You will have the medals in harmony, rhythm, and violin."

Mr. Sousa looked at Philip and smiled. "Does that seem fair to you?" he asked.

Philip nodded. He would have been happy with one of the medals. And he had won all five! Three was right in the middle.

"There is a very nice number." He looked at his father and grinned. "A very nice number."

Philip Changes His Mind

JOHN ESPUTA was a stern teacher. He often became excited and cross. One Saturday, when Philip went for his lesson, he found Mr. Esputa unusually cross.

When Philip walked into the room, he could tell at once that something was wrong. Mr. Esputa was lying in a hammock.

"I hope you have practiced hard," he said. "I don't feel well today, and I can't put up with any poor playing."

Philip quietly took his violin and bow out of their case. He spread out his music on the music rack and held up his bow to play. He had practiced hard, but was sure that he couldn't please Mr. Esputa. At last he started to play.

"No! No!" shouted John Esputa. "Not that way. You're sawing away like a carpenter."

Again Philip started to play.

"Too slow! Too slow!" shouted the teacher. "If you don't know how to play the piece, why don't you say so?"

Philip bit his lip. He turned back to the beginning again. He hadn't played the piece slowly because he didn't know it. He had played it slowly because he thought that was the way it should be played. If Mr. Esputa wanted him to play it fast, he would play it fast.

"Stop! Stop!" John Esputa sat up in his hammock. "You know that's much too fast."

Philip started the piece once more. It seemed to him that the lesson never would end. He glanced at the clock on the wall. Fifteen minutes until ten. Fifteen minutes more to go!

"Draw a long bow," John Esputa shouted from his hammock. "A long bow."

"I'm drawing the bow as long as I can," Philip answered. He could feel his cheeks getting red. He glanced at the clock again. Fourteen minutes until ten. Only one minute had passed.

"What?" John Esputa jumped up from his hammock. "Don't argue with me," he shouted. "Just do what I tell you to do."

"But I *am* drawing the bow as long as I can," Philip insisted.

John Esputa picked up a bow that was lying on the table. It was an expensive bow that he had bought only the week before.

"Look!" Then with a sweeping motion, he showed Philip how he wanted him to draw the bow. In his excitement he hadn't noticed how close he was standing to the stove.

Crack! The slender bow hit the stove and broke in two pieces.

58

"Get out!" John Esputa was so angry he didn't stop to think what he was doing or saying. "Get out, I tell you. Get out!"

Philip was angry, too. He'd go, all right, and never come back. He put his violin quickly in its case and hurried out of the room as fast as he could go.

"How can I face Papa?" he wondered. "All that money wasted!"

Philip walked along, with his head down. Just outside his own home, he almost ran into his father. Mr. Sousa knew at once that something was wrong. "What's the trouble, Philip?" he asked as they went into the house.

"Oh, that Mr. Esputa!" Philip's eyes filled with tears, but he wouldn't cry. "I never want to see him or his old school again."

Philip and his father went into the living room and sat down. Then Philip told his father everything that had happened.

60

"Well," said Mr. Sousa. "I suppose he must have been feeling sick. You know people often are cross when they aren't well."

"I know," Philip agreed, "but that's no excuse. It wasn't my fault that he was sick. If he didn't feel well, he shouldn't have tried to give me a lesson. When he broke his bow, you would have thought I was the one who did it. He didn't have to act like that."

"I know," said Mr. Sousa. "He shouldn't have acted that way. But he did—and there's nothing that you or I can do about it. He gets angry easily, but I imagine he's sorry afterward."

"He never says he's sorry," said Philip.

"Probably not," said Mr. Sousa. "Many musicians are excitable. They know how music should be played, and they can't bear to have someone play it wrong. You'll have to learn to take your teachers as they are. Learn what you can from them and forget the rest."

"I don't care," Philip said stubbornly. "I don't want to take any more lessons from him—ever."

Mr. Sousa looked very serious. "Well, I suppose, then, that you don't want to be a musician. You'll never be one, you know, unless you take lessons and do what your teacher tells you."

Mr. Esputa's angry voice was still ringing in Philip's ears. "Then I won't be a musician," he decided. "If I have to take lessons from Mr. Esputa, I just won't be a musician."

Mr. Sousa walked back and forth across the room, his hands behind his back. "You know, Philip," he said, "you will have to learn some kind of trade or profession. If you don't want to be a musician, what do you think you'd like to be?"

Philip couldn't answer. As long as he could remember, he had wanted to be a musician. He loved to play his violin. He loved to play other instruments, too, especially the cymbals and alto horn. Until today, he never had thought of being anything except a musician.

He walked over to the window and looked out. What would he like to be?

Just then a boy went by, carrying a large loaf of bread. Seeing the bread made Philip think of the bakery shop that he passed every day on his way to school. The windows of the shop were always full of cakes and pies and sweet rolls. The shop itself was filled with the wonderful odor of fresh, warm bread.

That would be a pleasant place to work. Charlie, the baker, was fat and jolly. He was nothing at all like Mr. John Esputa. Why not learn to be a baker? That would be a good trade. Instead of spending long hours practicing, he could be a baker and spend the rest of his life surrounded by good things to eat.

Philip turned quickly to his father. "Papa," he cried, "I know. I want to be a baker."

"A baker?" Mr. Sousa looked surprised and hurt. "Are you sure, Philip?"

"Yes." Philip nodded. "Yes, I'm sure. I'd rather be a baker than anything else."

"Very well." Mr. Sousa hurried to put on his coat. "If you want to be a baker, I'll see what I can do about it. Help is hard to get, and Charlie may be glad to have you, even though you are young. I'll try to arrange something."

Philip hadn't expected his father to act so quickly. About one minute ago, Philip had announced that he wanted to be a baker. Now Mr. Sousa was leaving the house.

"Where are you going, Papa?" Philip called after him. "Can't I come with you?"

"No, you stay here," Mr. Sousa called back over his shoulder. "I'll be back soon."

The Bakery Shop

HALF an hour later Mr. Sousa was home again. "It's all settled," he said to Philip. "I have talked with Charlie. He'll teach you to be a baker. You can start Monday evening. He wants you to be there by eight o'clock."

Philip was so excited that he could scarcely eat his supper Monday evening. It seemed to him that eight o'clock never would come. At seven-thirty, he hurried to the bakery shop.

Charlie, his wife, and the other workers in the shop were very kind to Philip. As he worked, he had a chance to see how pies, cookies, cake, and bread were made.

Philip liked the bread-making best. Charlie put the dough into big wooden troughs. After it had risen, he let Philip help him knead it. When it was time to shape the dough into big loaves,

Charlie took it out of the troughs and did the work himself.

Philip liked everything about the bakery shop. He was glad that he had decided to be a baker.

At last Charlie put the bread in the oven. "Now it's time for forty winks," he said. "Catch!" He threw a folded blanket to Philip.

Philip caught the blanket and looked around him, bewildered. What was he supposed to do?

In a few seconds he found out. Charlie and the other workmen spread their blankets in the big troughs where the bread had been mixed, crawled in and settled themselves for a nap. Philip, feeling a little foolish, put his blanket in a trough, too, and climbed in.

As he pulled the blanket up around him, he giggled to himself. He wondered what his friends at school would think if they could see him sleeping in a bread-dough trough. "Why, it's almost like sleeping in a canoe," he thought.

67

He turned back and forth, trying to get comfortable. The trough might be fun to sleep in, but it wasn't very soft. It wasn't very wide either. Philip found that he had to lie flat on his back, stiff and straight as a poker.

In spite of the uncomfortable trough, Philip was asleep in a very short time. Then, when it seemed he had scarcely closed his eyes, the baker was tugging at his arm. "Time to get up. The bread is ready to take out of the oven."

Philip helped to load the wagon, then went out with the driver to deliver the bread. It was early in the morning. No one was on the streets, and even the houses looked sound asleep.

The driver let Philip sit on his side of the seat and hold the reins. Philip felt very grown-up. He wished that Edward could see him driving Nick, the baker's horse. Soon, however, Philip realized that he wasn't really driving Nick. The horse stopped and started all by himself.

Nick knew all the customers and exactly where to stop for each delivery. He knew when it was time to go home, too. When the last loaf of bread had been delivered, he threw back his head with a snort, and headed for the shop.

It was eight o'clock when the horse stopped in front of the bakery. Philip's first night of work was over. He walked home quickly and found the family already at the breakfast table.

Mrs. Sousa looked at him anxiously. "Oh, Philip, you look so tired!" she said. "Tinnie, run into the kitchen and bring Philip's breakfast. It's in the warming oven."

Tinnie was back in a moment with her brother's plate. "What did you do, Philip?" she asked. "Did you eat lots of cookies?"

Mr. Sousa was watching Philip closely, but he asked no questions.

Philip took a mouthful of his egg before he answered his sister. "I could have had anything

I wanted," he boasted. "But I ate only one cookie and two pieces of warm bread. You should have seen me driving the horse!"

George put down his fork with a clatter. "I want to be a baker, too!" he said. "May I, Papa? May I go with Philip this evening?"

Everyone laughed as Mr. Sousa shook his head. "No, George. One baker in the family is enough. Maybe you will be our musician."

Philip looked at his father quickly. Mr. Sousa was busy eating again. Philip pushed back his plate. He slowly climbed the stairs to his room. He knew that his father was disappointed in him.

After Philip had changed his clothes, he hurried to school. Somehow school seemed very long that day. Sleeping in a bread-dough trough hadn't been exactly restful.

Usually arithmetic was one of Philip's favorite subjects. But today he wasn't interested.

Miss Johnson asked him to work a problem

that she had written on the blackboard. He put down some figures, but the answer was wrong.

"Oh, Philip," said Miss Johnson kindly. "You have made a mistake."

Instead of working the problem over, Philip shrugged his shoulders and went to his seat.

Miss Johnson was surprised, but she didn't scold Philip. She called on Edward, who worked the problem correctly.

When Edward went to his seat again, he whispered to Philip, "What's the matter? That was an easy problem." Philip didn't answer.

Two boys in Philip's class were waiting for him when he came out of school that afternoon. "Hey, Phil!" one of them called. "How about pitching for us this afternoon? You aren't going to music school any more, are you?"

Philip shook his head and walked away from the boys. He didn't feel like doing anything.

After supper that evening Philip went back to

the bakery again. He found the work much harder than it had been the night before. When it was time to take his midnight nap, he was too tired to think about the trough's being hard and narrow. He went to sleep in a second.

Early next morning he helped to load the wagon again and went out with the delivery man. Then at eight o'clock he hurried home.

All the Sousas were very quiet when they ate breakfast that morning. Both Mr. Sousa and his wife had worried looks on their faces. Tinnie set her brother's breakfast in front of him without saying a word.

Only George was brave enough to start talking. "Did you drive the horse again, Philip?" he asked eagerly. Philip only nodded in reply.

After breakfast Philip started to school without bothering to change his clothes. The last bell rang before he reached the school building, but he didn't care.

Philip didn't learn much of anything at school that day. All day long, he was so sleepy that he could scarcely keep his eyes open.

In the geography class several pupils gave reports on interesting things to see in Europe. Usually Philip held up his hand almost constantly during a lesson of this kind.

Today Philip just sat quietly, with his elbows propped on his desk and his head in his hands. At the end of the class, Miss Johnson walked back to his desk. She touched his shoulder. "Are you sick?" she asked.

Philip roused up enough to say, "No, Miss Johnson." Then he put his head down on his desk and went sound asleep.

That evening he returned to the bakery, wondering how he could stay awake.

The baker, who at first had been kind, now acted like a different man. He scolded Philip. He acted as bad as Mr. Esputa!

The baker's wife acted differently, too. When the baby cried, she snapped at Philip, "Here, you, go upstairs and rock the cradle."

Philip was completely worn out when he climbed the stairs. As soon as he sat down beside the baby, he went sound asleep.

"Wake up!" The baker's wife shook him. "Can't you hear the baby crying beside you?"

Philip was sure that nothing, not even a cannon, could keep him awake now. He never quite

remembered loading the wagon that third morning or making the deliveries. He couldn't even remember walking home. When he got into the house, he sat down in the first chair that he could find and went sound asleep.

The family was eating breakfast in the dining room. Tinnie jumped up to get Philip's breakfast, but Philip didn't come to breakfast. Finally Mrs. Sousa pushed back her chair and went into the living room to find him. Mr. Sousa followed close behind her.

Philip didn't hear his mother and father come in. There he sat, with his head slumped down and his legs sprawled out in front of him.

Mr. Sousa reached Philip first. He put his hand gently on Philip's shoulder. "Philip!" he called. "Philip, wake up!" Philip opened his eyes, but he hardly knew where he was.

"Give him some breakfast and put him to bed," Mr. Sousa said to his wife.

Philip stirred and tried to sit up. "I suppose you still want to be a baker," said his father.

"No!" Philip moaned. "I'd rather die than be a baker." He rubbed his eyes and blinked.

"Then," said Mr. Sousa, "you'd better make up with John Esputa and start your music lessons again. No job is easy, unless you're doing something that you really want to do."

Philip nodded. He knew that his father was right. He looked at his violin, resting on the shelf beside his father's trombone. It seemed like an old friend, waiting for him.

Philip could scarcely wait to rest the violin under his chin again, to feel the bow in his hand and to run his fingers over the strings. He hadn't touched his violin for three days. Suddenly he realized how much he had missed it.

Philip and the
President

FOR SEVERAL years now, there had been war. This war, which was known as the War between the States, was being fought between the North and the South. It had started in 1861, shortly after Abraham Lincoln became President.

The war years were very hard on the Sousa family and on all other families. Mr. Sousa was too old to take part in the war, and all his sons were too young.

Mr. Sousa kept on playing in the Marine Band. Every day or so he went to the Marine Barracks for rehearsal. Some members of the band were in the army, so there were fewer players than before. Therefore, it was important that each player work hard for the good of the band.

The war made Washington seem like a different place to Philip. Most of his older friends were taking part in the war. Some were fighting with the North and others with the South.

Often Philip went along with Mr. Sousa to the Marine Barracks. He was proud of his father and liked to hear the Marine Band practice. He was still taking lessons on the violin, but he was interested in band instruments, too.

Everyone in the band knew Philip. They knew that he played the violin and that he was interested in other instruments.

The members of the Marine Band called Philip Question Box. They gave him this nickname because he was always asking questions. Philip didn't care what they called him so long as they let him come to rehearsal.

Often during rehearsal the members of the

band let Philip hold their instruments. They let him practice for a few minutes on the alto horn, the trombone, or the drums. Sometimes they showed him the sheet music that they were following. Then he would try to see whether he could read and follow the notes.

One day, when the band was practicing, Philip sat down next to Mr. McCann, who played the alto horn. He sat close beside him and watched him finger the keys as he followed the music.

"Well, Question Box," said Mr. McCann when the band stopped to rest. "What questions are rattling around in your head today?"

Philip grinned. "None today," he said. "I've run out of questions."

Mr. McCann looked surprised. "I guess you've been too busy going to music school and taking lessons on your violin," he said. "Your father says that you also are learning to play the cymbals and the triangle and even—" he picked up his horn and gave a little toot— "even the alto horn. Here!" He handed the horn to Philip. "Let's see what you can do."

Philip picked up a sheet of Mr. McCann's music and put it on the rack. He put the horn to his lips. Then he began to play.

In a few minutes all the men in the band were listening. Even Mr. Weber, the leader of the band, came to listen.

"Say, Mr. Sousa, your son is good," he said.

80

"Hear the Sousa boy play that horn!"

"Not bad for a ten-year-old."

"Better be careful, McCann. He'll take your job away from you!"

Later Mr. Weber congratulated Philip. "Your father has told me about you," he said. "He says that you can play a number of instruments. Which one do you like best?"

Philip didn't know what to say. He had never thought about which one he liked best. "I like all of them," he said.

"Well, there is only one cure for that," said Mr. Weber. "You'll have to become a band leader. Then you can work with all of them."

Usually Philip was more interested in the musicians than in their leader. But this afternoon he was especially interested in Mr. Weber.

Philip watched him use his right hand to hold his baton and to beat time.

He watched the movement closely. Down

and up for 2/4 time. Down, right and up for 3/4 time. Down, right, left and up for 4/4 time.

Philip also watched Mr. Weber use his left hand to "talk" to the musicians.

"Sh! Softly. Softly." Mr. Weber moved his left hand as if he were patting a puppy. "Gently. Gently. Softer. Softer."

"Your turn! Your turn!" Mr. Weber extended his left hand toward the French horns.

"Come! Come!" Mr. Weber waved his left hand at the trumpets. "Louder! Louder!"

Philip looked at the men in the band. He noticed that each man was using both of his hands to play his instrument.

Philip looked at Mr. Weber more closely. "Why, he's using both of his hands, too," he thought, "just as all the players are." Philip threw back his head and laughed. "I guess he's playing an instrument, too." Philip was delighted with this idea. "He's playing the biggest instrument in the whole world. He's really play-ing a BAND!"

Philip leaned back in his chair and listened to the band play "Londonderry Air." This was one of his favorite pieces.

"Now I know what instrument I like best," he whispered to himself. "I like the BAND best. It's the biggest instrument in the world. And it's the most exciting, too."

One afternoon when Philip went to rehearsal with his father, Mr. Weber wanted to see him. "Philip," he said, "I have a problem. We're going to play a special program on the White House lawn tonight and want our music to sound its very best. Mr. McCann is ill and can't be with us to play his horn."

Mr. Weber shook his head. "We need some-one to take his place," he said, "but we can't find anyone. All the men who used to help us out in an emergency are in the army now. The war has been going on for three years, and there aren't many musicians left around here."

Mr. Weber smiled at the ten-year-old boy. "Philip, you seem to be the only person left in Washington who can take Mr. McCann's place," he said. "Will you play for us tonight?"

Philip was far too surprised to answer.

Play Mr. McCann's horn?

Play in the Marine Band?

PLAY AT THE WHITE HOUSE?

"Oh, yes, sir!" Philip found his voice. "Thank you very much. I'll—I'll do my best."

Mr. Weber put his arm around Philip's shoulders and thanked him. "First we'll practice all the pieces that we plan to play tonight," he said. "Then you run over to see Mr. Wilson, our tailor, about getting a uniform. You must wear a uniform, of course."

Philip sat down and practiced playing all the pieces with the other members of the band. He played his part well, just as Mr. McCann would have played it. At the end of the rehearsal, he hurried to Mr. Wilson's workshop.

"Mr. Wilson! Mr. Wilson!"

"Eh? Oh, it's you, Philip. Come in."

"Mr. Wilson, I'm going to play with the band this evening and—" Philip stopped for breath— "I—I need a uniform. Mr. Weber said——"

Mr. Wilson looked at Philip. "You? A marine uniform for you? The heavens help us! Tell Mr. Weber I'm a tailor—not a magician."

"But, Mr. Wilson, we're playing at the White House tonight, and——"

"I know. I know." Mr. Wilson pointed to a rack filled with uniforms. "I've been working on those uniforms all day. I've been cleaning and pressing them, trying to get them ready for to-night. The men will come for them soon."

Philip looked at the blue trousers and red coats. "They're beautiful, Mr. Wilson."

"Beautiful? Of course they're beautiful. But just standing here and saying they're beautiful doesn't help us find one to fit you."

Philip looked over the uniforms more closely. He picked up one of the coat sleeves and ran his fingers over the gold braid trimming. Then he looked at the trousers.

"I have a good pair of blue trousers," he said. "They're almost this shade. All that I really need is a red coat."

"Trousers, eh?" Mr. Wilson looked a little encouraged. "You need a red coat. A red coat. Well, let's see, now." He crossed the room and opened a big chest. "We have some old coats in this chest. I wonder——"

Mr. Wilson took a coat out of the chest and shook it. "Well, one thing's certain," he said, "it's easier to make a little coat out of a big one, than a big coat out of a little one. Come and let me measure you."

Mr. Wilson measured Philip's arms, shoulders and waist very carefully.

Philip was so excited about playing with the Marine Band that he could scarcely believe it was true. Every minute he could hear the pieces of music ringing in his ears.

He felt certain that he could follow the music without any trouble. He could almost see the notes dance before his eyes. He knew how the fingering should go.

"Now run along," Mr. Wilson said at last. He pulled his spectacles down to the end of his nose and looked at Philip over the frames. "You'll probably want to do some more practicing before you have to go to the concert. I'll work on your coat and try to have it ready around six o'clock. See you then."

Mr. Sousa was waiting for Philip. He helped his son carry the big alto horn to their house. His eyes shone with fatherly pride.

When they reached home, Mrs. Sousa called, "Philip, I have an errand——"

"No, Mamma," declared Mr. Sousa firmly, "not today. Philip has to practice some music. He is going to play in the Marine Band concert on the White House lawn tonight."

Mrs. Sousa was surprised. So were other members of the family. Philip didn't try to explain. He just took the alto horn and music up to his room and began to practice. Everyone in the family listened to him.

At six o'clock Philip returned to Mr. Wilson's workshop, wearing his blue trousers. Then he put on his own specially-made red marine coat with gold braid trimming.

"It's beautiful! Beautiful!" exclaimed Philip as he stared at the coat. "And it's exactly like Papa's. Even the buttons are the same! You're a wonderful tailor, Mr. Wilson. You're really a magician. A tailor-magician."

"You like it, eh?" Mr. Wilson looked pleased, too. "I never thought that old coat would go to a concert again—and here it is, going off to the White House. And you'd better go, too, young fellow, if you don't want to be late."

Late? He couldn't be late! He took one last look at the coat. Then he hurried toward the door. "Thank you, Mr. Wilson. Thank——"

"Hurry, son." Mr. Wilson gave him a little push. "You can thank me tomorrow. Or next week. But now you must hurry."

When Philip arrived at the White House gates, his father was waiting for him.

Mr. Sousa turned Philip around and around to look at him. "You look fine, Philip."

Philip nodded. He was sure that he never had been so excited before.

"Papa, may I ask you something?"

"Yes, Philip."

"Will President Lincoln attend the concert?"

Mr. Sousa shook his head. "I doubt it, Philip, and I'm very sorry. President Lincoln has to settle many problems these days. He works all day and far into the night. It's too bad that he can't get away from his troubles for a little while—but he can't."

Philip and his father walked across the White House lawn. They took their places in the bandstand. People came from every direction and filled all the seats in front of the bandstand. They laughed and talked. The musicians tuned their instruments. Philip looked out over the sea of faces before him. His knees were shaking with excitement.

Then Mr. Weber, stiff and straight, walked to the front of the platform. Suddenly everyone was quiet. He raised his baton.

And the concert started.

When the band was halfway through its second number, Philip happened to glance toward the White House. He noticed the doors open behind the big white columns, and saw a tall, lean figure walk slowly down the steps.

"Why, it's President Lincoln!" Philip was so surprised he almost said the words aloud.

Philip looked at the people on the lawn. They sat with their backs to the White House entrance and hadn't seen the President. Philip looked at the other members of the band. They hadn't seen the President, either.

"I'm the only one who has seen him," Philip said to himself. "The only one."

President Lincoln walked around the edge of the crowd until he came to the side of the bandstand. He stood behind a big tree, and was almost completely hidden from the crowd. But Philip saw him plainly.

"I guess he just came out for a little walk," Philip said to himself. "I guess he doesn't want anyone bothering him."

Philip looked at Mr. Lincoln. His cheeks were furrowed. His eyes looked hazy. His back was stooped. He looked tired and sad.

At that moment Mr. Lincoln happened to see Philip. At first he looked surprised. Then slowly he began to smile. The deep lines in his cheeks disappeared. His eyes twinkled. Finally his whole face was smiling. Philip was sure it was the kindest and the most wonderful smile that he had ever seen.

When Philip noticed that the President was watching him, he sat up straight, threw back his head and tilted his horn into the air.

This amused Mr. Lincoln. He threw back his head, too, and began to laugh. Then he looked at Philip, put his finger gently to his lips and shook his head.

Philip understood. The President didn't want anyone to know that he was there.

Mr. Lincoln leaned against the tree and listened to the music for about half an hour. Once when Philip glanced at him, the President stood up straight and saluted. He ended the salute with a friendly wave of the hand. Then he turned and walked back across the lawn.

"He was here only a little while," Philip said to himself, "but I made him smile. I made him throw back his head and laugh. Maybe he feels better now than he did before he came. Maybe I helped him a little.

"Anyway," Philip smiled to himself, "it's fun to have a secret with the President of the United States—a secret with Mr. Lincoln!"

Marching in the Parade

In 1865 the War between the States came to an end. The Northern armies won, and a great celebration was held in Washington to welcome the returning soldiers.

The people in Washington cleaned the streets and decorated them with flags and bunting. They put up signs saying: "Welcome Home." "Welcome to the Nation's Heroes." Every street had some kind of decoration.

When the day came, Mrs. Sousa decided to stay at home with the smallest children. "I'm glad that the war is over," she said. "And I don't need to see a parade to make me happy."

Tinnie and one of the girls in her class started for the parade bright and early. They took George and Tony with them.

Mr. Sousa and Philip went early, too, but already the sidewalks were crowded. In front of the White House school children were standing on either side of the street.

The girls wore white dresses and the boys wore duck trousers and blue jackets. Some of the girls had red, white, and blue rosettes pinned on their dresses. Others had bouquets of flowers that they planned to toss at the soldiers when they came marching by.

Philip and his father found seats in a stand that had been built in front of the White House. Their seats were in the front row, where they could see everything clearly. They couldn't have found a better place.

The crowd got thicker and thicker. "Whew!" Mr. Sousa wiped his forehead with his handkerchief. "It's going to be hot today. I'm glad that we found these good seats. It will be easy to wait here."

But Philip didn't find waiting easy. He thought the parade would never start.

Finally there was a rumbling sound down the street, and the first group of soldiers appeared. "There's Meade," someone called out. Immediately everyone began to shout, "Hurrah for Meade! Hurrah for General Meade!"

One group of soldiers after another passed by, and Philip became very restless. He thought that the long lines of soldiers would never end. Somehow the celebration wasn't nearly so exciting as he had expected it would be.

Suddenly, down the street came an officer on a wild-looking horse. The rider had no hat, and his long, light brown hair was blowing in the wind. He held one hand in the air.

In an instant the whole crowd was panic-stricken. "Who is he?" asked a man. "He'll be dashed to pieces."

"We'll all be dashed to pieces," shouted a lady who was seated near by.

Then everyone cried out at once.

"Stop him! Stop him!"

"We'll all be killed."

"Can't someone do something?"

"Stop him! Stop him!"

When the horse and rider reached a spot in front of the stand, the horse reared up with the rider on its back. There it stood for a moment, with its head held high, its eyes wild with excitement, and its mane blowing in the breeze. When it came down, Philip gasped. He was sure that both the horse and the rider would come tumbling into the stand. He had never been so frightened before.

"Who's the rider?" someone called out. "Who's the man on the horse?"

"It's Custer," shouted an officer, standing up in his chair. "It's General Custer."

In an instant Mr. Sousa stood on his chair, too. He turned around and faced the crowd. "It's all right," he shouted as loudly as he could. "It's all right. Sit down, everyone. Sit down! If it's Custer, we don't have to worry. No horse has ever run away with him yet—and I don't think one ever will."

Somehow Mr. Sousa managed to make himself heard above the shouting. Suddenly the crowd became quiet. The panic was over.

"Look, now!" Mr. Sousa called, pointing toward the street. There, calm and steady, sat General Custer on his horse.

"You see—" Mr. Sousa smiled at Philip— "that horse is just as gentle as a parson's nag on Sunday. At first I was frightened. But when someone said that the man was Custer, I knew there was no need to worry."

He put his arm around Philip's shoulder.

"General Custer doesn't ride a horse because he has to," he said knowingly. "He rides a horse because he can."

From then on, the parade seemed to be more interesting. Bands began to play, and there were many more things to see.

A troop of cavalry came by, and the people began to cheer. Philip shouted at the top of his voice and threw his cap into the air.

The cavalry officers wore beautiful uniforms. They sat erect on their high-stepping horses and looked straight ahead. Their sabers glistened in the sunlight, and their red scarves fluttered around their necks.

The horses seemed to keep time to the music, and to Philip each one seemed to say, "Look at me. Look at me. I'm marching. I'm marching in the parade."

A soldier came by with a raccoon clinging to

his shoulder. The raccoon held its head close to the soldier's cheek and looked at the crowd with bright, piercing eyes. Like the horses, he seemed to be saying to Philip, "Look at me. I'm marching. I'm marching in the parade."

Some of the soldiers marched by with mules and donkeys. Some of them led cows and goats and sheep. Some had dogs tagging along faithfully at their heels. One old pack horse had a crowing rooster perched on its back. The people began to laugh. But to Philip each animal seemed to be saying, "Look at me. I'm marching. I'm marching in the parade."

The marching music was almost more than Philip could stand. He felt as if he just had to get out on the street and march. He tapped his feet to keep time with the music. He whistled and hummed some of the songs that he knew. He wanted to be able to say, "Look at me. I'm marching. I'm marching in the parade, too."

102

A few minutes later one of the marching soldiers looked up and recognized Mr. Sousa. "Antonio! Tony!" he shouted. "Tony, how are you?"

Mr. Sousa jumped up from his seat and reached over the railing. "Sam Dickson," he cried. "Sam, I'm mighty glad to see you."

Then, all of a sudden, Mr. Sousa jumped down from the stand and started to walk along beside his old friend. "Sam," he said, patting Mr. Dickson on the back, "how have you been? We had no idea what had happened to you. Man, it's great to see you alive and well."

"There were times when I didn't think I'd ever see Washington again," Sam said. "But the war's over at last, and here I am. It's wonderful to be home once more."

Philip followed his father. He jumped down and hurried into the street. At first he found that his steps were too short for keeping up with the soldiers. He began to take longer and longer steps until they matched the steps of the marching soldiers perfectly. Then he threw back his shoulders and shouted, "Left! Right! Left!— Left! Right! Left!"

Now Philip began to have the time of his life. He marched down the street beside a long row of soldiers. He took longer steps than he had ever taken before, but he was having fun. Then, without thinking, he shouted, "Look at me! I'm marching. I'm marching, too."

All the people along the street cheered. They were happy because the war was over. The soldiers were back. Philip was happy, too. He was glad that the war was over. And he was happy because he was marching in the parade.

But Philip had no one to tell about the wonderful feeling he had inside. Instead, he began to hum the tune that the band was playing. It was one of his favorite marches.

He threw back his head and laughed. The

march tune was saying all the things that he felt. It was saying these things to everyone.

Philip nodded his head slowly. Sometimes music could say things far better than words. And on a day like this, filled with happiness, one march was better than a thousand speeches.

"You're marching," the band seemed to say to Philip. "You're marching, too!"

The Borrowed Shirt

PHILIP didn't spend all of his time practicing music. He liked to play baseball, too. He was one of the pitchers on a team called The Navy Yard Boys.

One day, after school, Philip saw the members of his team huddled together on the playground. "Hey!" Joe, the captain, shouted to him. "You haven't forgotten the game, have you?"

The game? For a minute Philip didn't know what game the captain was talking about. Then he remembered. This game was to be the big one of the year. The Navy Yard Boys were to play the Capitol Hill team. Philip's heart sank.

Today also was the big day of the year at the music school. Philip dug his toe into the dirt, trying to decide what to do.

At last he shook his head and said, "Gee, I'm sorry. I can't play today. The orchestra at Mr. Esputa's school is giving a concert tonight and I'm the soloist. I have to get home early. I have to get dressed and——"

The whole team crowded around Philip.

"You can't let us down," said Edward. "The game will be over long before it's time for the concert. Come on and pitch the game for us. Please, Philip."

"You're the best pitcher we've got."

"If the Capitol Hill team beats us, we'll never hear the end of it."

"The game won't last long. We'll win it before Capitol Hill even gets started."

"Come on, Philip. You'll get home in plenty of time for the concert."

"It's going to be a good game—the best one this year. We need you to pitch."

Philip was tempted to give in. He had looked forward all year to playing this game. The Capitol Hill boys thought, because they lived near the Capitol, that they were better than anyone else. Some of them had teased Philip about playing the violin. Now he wanted to show them that he could play baseball, too.

"Aw, come on, Philip."

Philip hesitated a minute. He already knew the music that he would play at the concert. Maybe he could pitch the game after all. Perhaps it wouldn't last long—only an hour or so. The Navy Yard Boys would beat the Capitol Hill team fast and send it on its way.

"All right." He held up his hands for the ball. "Come on. Let's go."

The game went on and on. The Capitol Hill team was strong and played a very good game.

Philip forgot about his music. He forgot about the concert. He forgot about the time.

At the end of the seventh inning, the score was nine to six in favor of Capitol Hill. Joe, the captain of the Navy Yard Boys, looked discouraged. He gathered his team together for a minute.

"Look, fellows!" he said, tapping his catcher's mitt. "Those boys are only three runs ahead. Just don't let them get any more. Thomas and Riley are the ones to watch. Be careful how you pitch to them, Philip. We can still win."

Philip nodded grimly. He took his place on the pitcher's mound. Edward tapped Philip on the shoulder as he ran to left field. "Keep them guessing," he said. "Be careful."

That is just what Philip did. First he pitched a high ball. Then he pitched a low ball. Then he sent a ball waist high. Capitol's batters struck out—one, two, three. There was a wild yell from the Navy boys as the last Capitol batter threw down his bat in disgust.

There was great excitement in the last half of the eighth inning while the Navy boys were batting. Edward was first batter up. He made a long two-base hit. Philip was the second batter, and he drove the ball just over the second baseman's head. He streaked for first base and beat the throw. The third batter was Joe, who hit a home run. Now the score was tied nine to nine.

The next Navy boy hit at every ball and struck out. The two players who followed hit slow rollers to the shortstop and were easy outs. A big groan came from the Navy team.

Both teams played very hard in the ninth inning, but all the players were tired. Philip went to the mound, scooped up a handful of dirt and rubbed his hands. He wound up slowly and carefully pitched the first ball. The batter swung at it with all his might, but didn't come close to hitting it. In the first half of the inning, the batters went down—one, two, three.

The Navy players now forgot about being tired. They still had a chance to win. The first Navy batter was Tom, one of the huskiest boys on the team. As the Capitol Hill pitcher looked at Tom, he became greatly rattled. Finally, he threw the ball, wondering what would happen.

Smack! Tom hit the ball squarely. He threw down his bat and fairly flew around the bases. All the Navy boys held their breath until he reached home plate. Then everyone yelled.

Joe rushed over to Tom and threw his arms around him. Edward shouted to Philip. "You pitched a wonderful game. We did it!"

Philip rubbed his hands together excitedly. "I never had so much fun!" he exclaimed. Suddenly he clapped both his hands to his mouth. "Oh, oh!" he said. "The concert!"

He started for home, hot and tired. He knew he wouldn't have time for supper, but he didn't mind. He was glad to go without eating, just to win the game.

As he passed a jewelry store, he glanced at a clock. Six-thirty! He was supposed to be at Mr. Esputa's at seven. He really would have to hurry to get dressed. "Gee—" he shook his head— "I'm late!"

When Philip reached home, he found the house in a state of confusion. His mother had become ill with a headache and was in bed. Tinnie was away on a visit. Mr. Sousa was at the

Marine Barracks. The younger children, left to themselves, were trying to get their own supper.

"Philip!" called Tony from the kitchen. "Come and help us get supper."

"I can't, Tony," Philip answered. "I have to get ready to go to the concert. I'm late now." He hurried on upstairs.

He got out his best suit, his new shoes and his clean socks. But when he looked for a clean white shirt, he couldn't find one. He almost called to his mother. "No, I mustn't," he said to himself. "She has one of her bad headaches, and I mustn't disturb her."

Philip didn't know what to do. He had to have a clean shirt, but he didn't know where to get one now. There were only twenty minutes left before the concert.

Philip decided to put his problem up to Mr. Esputa. He ran all the way to the music school and told Mr. Esputa.

"No shirt?" Mr. Esputa stared at him. "But why do you tell me this now—fifteen minutes before the concert? Why are you so late?"

As quickly as he could, Philip told him about the game and why he hadn't had time to look for his shirt. For once Mr. Esputa was too worried to get angry. "A shirt? A shirt?"

For a moment he wandered around as if he expected to find a clean shirt somewhere in his office. Then he happened to think of his home. "Run over and tell my wife to give you one of my shirts," he said.

Fortunately, Mr. Esputa lived next door to his school. Philip ran across the little courtyard and told Mrs. Esputa what he wanted.

Mrs. Esputa was a sweet, good-natured woman. She rushed upstairs and came back with one of Mr. Esputa's best linen shirts.

Philip grabbed the shirt and ran into the bedroom to put it on. When he came out a few minutes later, Mrs. Esputa bent over laughing. "You look so funny," she said.

The shirt hung on him like a sack. The collar was three sizes too big for him. The cuffs covered his hands like little muffs.

Mrs. Esputa took another look at him and began to laugh again. Philip laughed, too. Then, suddenly, they both realized that something had to be done, and done quickly.

Mrs. Esputa ran from the room and came back carrying a pincushion. "The only way I know how to make the shirt smaller is with pins."

First she pinned up the body of the shirt all the way around. Then she pinned up the sleeves and the collar.

Philip ran across the courtyard again, scarcely allowing himself to breathe. When he got to school, the other members of the orchestra had already taken their places.

The stage was crowded, but Philip finally

managed to reach his place near the center. Mr. Esputa raised his baton. The orchestra played a few bars. Then Philip put his violin against his shoulder and began to play.

After Philip began to play, he forgot all about the shirt. He forgot all about the ball game. He didn't think about anything except his violin and the piece that he was playing.

He played well. The piece was a lively tune, and everyone seemed to enjoy it.

The music went very fast in one place. Philip had to move his arm back and forth with quick, short strokes.

Playing this way was hard on the shirt. Some of the pins began to come loose. One pricked Philip on his neck, another stuck him on his elbow. Soon the collar came undone and worked itself up to Philip's chin. Then the sleeves began to slip down. They slipped lower and lower until they covered Philip's hands.

Philip tried to stretch his arms to work the sleeves back. He tried to wiggle his wrists to get the cuffs out of the way. Nothing seemed to help. Finally his right hand became so mixed up with a cuff that he had to stop playing.

The people in the audience laughed and laughed at Philip and the baggy shirt. Even the other members of the orchestra laughed, although they tried very hard not to.

Philip dashed off the stage. He never had been so embarrassed in his life! He took off his coat and threw it on a chair. He started to unbutton his shirt, eager to get rid of it. Just then Mr. Esputa stormed into the room.

"Well!" Mr. Esputa glared at Philip. "You had to play baseball this afternoon! You should have been preparing for the concert instead!"

"I know! I know!" Philip had never felt so miserable. "I'm sorry, Mr. Esputa," he said. "Really I am."

118

"Humph!" Mr. Esputa looked at Philip. The shirt was hanging below Philip's coat. The collar almost covered his chin. The cuffs hung loosely over his fingers.

John Esputa began to laugh. "Well," he said, "if you don't want to be a musician, you can always be a clown."

Philip knew that he looked funny, but he didn't feel like laughing. He hurried home.

As he opened the front door, he listened for a moment. Tinnie's voice came from the back of the house. She was talking with the children.

Philip closed the door quietly and tiptoed upstairs. He noticed a light coming from his mother's room. He looked in the door and whispered softly, "Are you awake, Mamma?"

"Yes, my son, come in," Mrs. Sousa answered. "How did the concert go?"

Philip sank to his knees and buried his head in the pillow. He cried and cried as his mother smoothed his hair silently. Then, bit by bit, he told the story of the borrowed shirt.

"Everything is all right, Philip," Mrs. Sousa said. "Everything is all right."

Later Philip crawled into bed. "I found out one thing today," he said to himself. "I can't mix work and play. From now on when it's time to work, I'll work hard. And when it's time to play, I'll play hard. But I'll never—never—never again try to mix the two."

Philip Plays
Happy Music

ONE DAY Mr. Esputa made an important announcement. "Next week," he said, "an unusual concert will be given here in Washington. It will be given by the Frankos, a family of five extremely talented children. I want all of you to hear them."

Each day from then on, Mr. Esputa said something about the Frankos. Philip looked forward to hearing them. He was sure that their program would be something special.

Philip told his father, mother, and Tinnie about the concert. Then, much to his surprise, Tinnie asked whether she could go, too.

"May I go to the concert with you, Philip?" she asked. "I'm not one of Mr. Esputa's pupils, but I would like to go anyway."

"Why, of course, you may go," answered Philip. "But don't expect me to wait for you if you're not ready. The concert is next Wednesday night. I want to go early to get a good seat."

"I'll be ready, Philip," said Tinnie. "You won't have to wait for me."

Finally the day of the concert arrived. Philip and Tinnie ate their supper early. When Philip was ready to start, Tinnie was waiting on the porch. They hurried to the concert hall.

Philip and Tinnie found good seats in the center of the second row. They were right down front, where they could see everyone on the stage. They could hear every note of the music.

Tinnie chatted as the people came in. "It must be exciting to give a concert," she said.

"Oh, I don't know," answered Philip in a bored

122

voice. "Papa doesn't get excited when the Marine Band gives a concert."

"But that's different!" said Tinnie. "He plays with the whole band. I mean it must be exciting to play alone. I'd be scared!"

"Well, I've never been scared when I've played a solo in Mr. Esputa's concerts," said Philip. "I've just thought about the music I was playing."

Just then the red velvet curtain opened.

"Oo-oo-oo-oo!" The audience was astounded to see a little boy on the stage.

Philip looked at his program. The first performer was Nahan Franko, seven years old.

As Philip glanced up, he wondered why Mr. Esputa had asked his pupils to come here. "Surely this little seven-year-old boy can't play," he said.

Nahan Franko raised his violin and began to play. The audience watched and listened as he played the first notes. Soon everyone realized that he was playing a very difficult piece of music. And he was playing it as well as a trained adult would play it.

Philip stared at the stage. At first he couldn't believe that the notes were coming from the little boy's violin. A few minutes later, he forgot all about the little violinist. All he could think about was the beautiful music that was coming from the violin.

Philip had never heard the music that Nahan played. He had never realized that a violin could sound so beautiful.

After Nahan finished playing, the other Franko children performed on various instruments. They all played especially well. When the concert was over, Philip thought that Nahan had played best of all.

As Philip and Tinnie started to leave the hall, Tinnie paused to talk with one of her friends. Philip walked on until he came to a big poster

124

hanging beside the door. The poster showed a picture of little Nahan playing his violin.

"Just think," said Philip, stopping to look at the picture. "He's only seven years old!"

Tinnie caught up with Philip. "Oh, Philip, I didn't mean to make you wait," she said.

Philip stood still and looked at the picture. "Seven years old!" he repeated. "Why, he's five years younger than I am!"

At last Philip noticed his sister. "Yes, five years younger," he said. "I'm really going to work from now on."

All the way home Philip kept thinking of the wonderful music he had heard. He began to hum the melodies. He kept on humming them as he got ready for bed.

Then, just as he blew out the light, Philip knew what he wanted to do. He wanted to compose a piece of music. He wanted to create a melody that was beautiful, just as beautiful as the music that he had heard at the hall. He would test the music on his violin to see whether he liked it.

Philip first tried to think of little bits of music that he could put together to make a new melody. He tried one bit of music after another on his violin, but not one of them sounded the way he wanted it to sound.

"Composing music is harder than I thought," Philip said to himself.

But Philip kept trying. More than anything else, he wanted to compose some music.

Suddenly, one afternoon, something happened. As Philip picked up his violin, he seemed to know a new tune. He wondered where it had come from, but he couldn't tell. It just seemed to be there, inside his head. Now he would try to play it.

Philip tucked his violin under his chin and started to play the tune softly. He felt that he must play the tune softly. Otherwise, he might frighten it away. He didn't want to do that.

"There!" smiled Philip, as he finished playing the tune. "Now it belongs to me."

Philip played the tune again, a little louder than before. It sounded even better than it had the first time. "Just think!" he cried. "It's all mine. And it's different from any melody that I've heard before."

To Philip the little tune seemed alive and friendly, like a new-born pet. "I must take care of it and help it to grow," he said as he played it again on his violin. "If I take care of it, it will grow into a fine piece of music."

Philip worked hard to make his melody grow. First he played a few notes one way. Then he played the sames notes another way. He played them over and over. Finally, when he was satisfied with them, he wrote them down in his music notebook.

At last Philip finished the piece of music. He was very happy, and rushed into another part of the house to play it for his mother.

"It's beautiful," she exclaimed. "And to think that you composed the piece all by yourself! I'm very proud of you."

Later in the day Philip played the piece of music for his brothers and sisters.

"Oh, I like that," exclaimed Tinnie. "What is the name of it?"

Philip looked surprised. "I haven't thought of a name yet," he said, "but I will."

"It makes me feel very gay," said Elise.

"It makes me want to march," said George.

"Me, too," said Louis, who was four years old. "Me, too." And he began to march back and forth across the room.

Soon his older brothers and sisters were marching behind him, humming and whistling Philip's tune.

"Music makes people do many things," Philip thought to himself. "It can make people laugh and sing and hum and whistle and march and dance. Music can make people happy."

Philip looked at his brothers and sisters. They were still marching around the room. "I hope more happy tunes pop into my head," he said. "I want to compose only happy music."

129

The Circus
Parade

A CIRCUS was coming! On the sides of buildings all over town there were big signs showing pictures of the circus. There were pictures of the large circus tents. There were pictures of clumsy elephants and roaring lions. There were pictures of women riding beautiful horses and acrobats hanging in midair.

The Sousa children were greatly excited. They talked about the circus all day long. They talked about it morning, noon, and night.

"I wish we would go!" exclaimed Tinnie one evening at supper. "Wouldn't it be wonderful if we could?" She looked at all her brothers and

130

sisters, seated around the table. By this time there were eight children in the family.

Then she looked at her father. "Oh, Papa, I'm sorry," she said quickly. "I know that we can't afford to buy eight tickets."

"Eight?" asked Mr. Sousa, pretending to feel hurt. "You can't leave Mamma and me out. If we can't afford to buy eight tickets, we might as well *not* afford to buy ten. Mamma and I, we like circuses, too."

"Ah," said Mrs. Sousa, "in Bavaria, when I was a girl, we had wonderful circuses."

"And in Spain," said Mr. Sousa, remembering, "the circuses—they were wonderful."

"And in America," said Philip, sounding exactly like his father, "the parades—they are wonderful. At least we can see the parade."

All the Sousas laughed. They had forgotten all about the parade. Why, it would be almost as good as the circus itself.

Everybody began to act silly. Tinnie and Elise jumped up from the table and began to dance a Bavarian folk dance that their mother had taught them. George and Tony began to sing an old Spanish song that the children had learned from their father. The baby, pounding on the table with his spoon, tried to keep time to the song.

"Children! Children!" Mrs. Sousa tried to look cross, but she couldn't keep from smiling. "Quit acting silly and finish your supper."

Mr. Sousa stood up at the head of the table. He tapped his water glass with a spoon. "I just wish to announce," he said, "that we don't need to buy tickets for a circus. We can see a circus free any time we wish. In a family like ours, we have a circus going on all the time."

Finally the day of the circus arrived. All the children got up early in the morning. Mrs. Sousa didn't have to call anyone for breakfast.

132

"Well," said Mr. Sousa, looking up from his morning paper. "We can't go to the circus, but the circus is coming to us. Here is a map of the city, showing where the parade will take place. It will pass right in front of our house."

All the children except the two smallest ones crowded around Mr. Sousa and the map.

"Will the parade really come by here?"

"Will it come right down this street?"

"What time will it come?"

"From what direction will it come?"

"Can we hear it coming?"

"Can we watch it from the sidewalk?"

"Can we watch it from an upstairs window?"

"Just a minute! Just a minute! I can't answer all of you at once." Mr. Sousa tried to rescue his paper. "Go back to the table and eat your breakfast. I'll read you what it says."

"Isn't that fine?" said Mrs. Sousa when he had finished. "We can stay right at home and see the

133

parade. We don't have to go some place else to see it. And I can go right on cooking," she added. "I won't have to stop until the parade reaches the front of the house."

Mr. Sousa looked at his wife. "Now, Mamma," he said, "do you have to work *all* the time? Can't you take a day off once in a while?"

Mrs. Sousa laughed. "When this family takes a day off from eating, I'll take a day off from cooking," she said. "Right now I must put some pies in the oven. Ten people may be rather hungry by suppertime tonight."

By the time breakfast was over, a few people had gathered in front of the house. By nine o'clock the sidewalk was crowded. By ten o'clock there was no room for anyone else.

At first George, Tony, and Elise ran in and out of the house. When the sidewalks became crowded, they had to spend more and more time in the house. Finally, when it was almost time for the parade, they came into the house and closed the door.

The two youngest children weren't interested, but all the others rushed upstairs and found places at the front bedroom windows. The smaller ones stood in front, and the older children at the back. From here everyone could look down on the street and get a good view.

"Yoo hoo!" the children called to some of their friends below. Their friends called back to them. Everything seemed very exciting.

"I feel like a fairy princess," said Elise with a smile. "I feel as if I'm locked up in a tower."

Philip looked down at the crowd. Even the yard was full of people now. "You're locked up, all right," he said. "I don't think you could get out of the house no matter what happened."

Mrs. Sousa looked over Philip's head. "Oh, dear," she said. "I hope the people down there don't ruin my beds of roses. I——"

"There comes the band!" shouted Philip. "Be quiet, everyone. It's coming!"

The parade was still four blocks away, but Philip's sharp ears had caught the sound. A few minutes later everyone else could hear the band, too. It was coming down the street, leading the parade. The crowd cheered.

The Sousa children leaned farther and farther out the front windows. Each one wanted to be the first to see the band.

"I see it! I see it!" each shouted at the same time. "It's coming! It's coming."

Everyone saw the band except Mrs. Sousa. She was busy pulling the children back. "Be careful," she cried. "You'll fall out the windows. Parade or no parade, don't lean out so far."

The band came nearer and nearer. At last it was directly in front of the house. Mrs. Sousa still watched her children, but felt somewhat relieved. Finally she, too, watched the parade.

136

"What a beautiful band!" shouted Philip, staring out the window. The bandsmen wore red and white uniforms trimmed with gold braid. They carried big brass instruments that flashed in the sunlight.

Philip couldn't take his eyes off the band. He watched it until the last man was out of sight. If Tony hadn't tugged at his sleeve, he might even have missed the clowns.

There were all kinds of clowns. Some were on stilts and walked by, almost as high as the Sousa children in the window.

After the clowns came animals in large red and yellow wagons. There were lions and tigers, zebras and leopards, gorillas and bears. Next came prancing horses and ponies with bright-colored plumes. Men and women rode by, smiling and waving from beautiful carriages.

Last of all in the parade came the elephants. They walked in a long line trunk-to-tail.

"Oh, look," cried Tony, "the elephants are holding hands."

Everyone laughed. It seemed funny to see the elephants marching in this way.

A few minutes later the last elephant walked by the house. People stood and watched it until it was out of sight. Then they rushed into the streets and hurried to their homes.

The big parade was over.

Philip Meets a Band Leader

AFTER THE parade everyone felt a little restless. Mrs. Sousa hurried to look at her pies, which were still in the oven. Tinnie went down the street to visit a friend. George, Tony, Elise, and Louis went outdoors to play.

Philip wandered restlessly from room to room, looking for something to do. He had thought that, if he saw the parade, he would be satisfied to miss the circus. But he wasn't. He wanted to go to the circus more than ever. He wanted to see and hear the band again.

The circus music rang in his ears. He hummed to himself the march tune that the band had

140

played. Then he whistled it softly to himself, over and over again.

At last he walked into the living room and picked up his violin. He wanted to see whether he could play the march tune from memory, just as the band had played it. Somehow the notes, one after another, fell into their proper places. Soon he was marching up and down the room, playing the circus music on his violin.

As Philip played, he became far less restless than he was before. Nothing satisfied him as much as playing his violin. At last he stopped playing the circus music and began to play one of his old favorite pieces.

Philip forgot about the time. The house was quiet, and no one came into the living room to bother him. He played on and on.

Suddenly he heard a loud knock at the door. He stopped playing and walked into the front hall. "I thought the peace and quiet couldn't last," he mumbled to himself. "I wonder who is out there."

Slowly he opened the door and looked out. He blinked and looked again. There, in front of him, was a member of the circus band. Philip recognized the red and white uniform at once.

But this was not all. Philip noticed that the man was wearing a big high hat with a stiff plume. Philip blinked again. This man wasn't a regular member of the circus band. He was the *leader* of the band.

Philip couldn't imagine what the man wanted, but at last he managed to say, "Hello."

The band leader seemed embarrassed, too. "I've been standing outside listening to someone playing beautiful music," he said. "Finally I decided to come in to see who it was." Just then he noticed that Philip was holding a violin. "Are you the one who has been playing?" he asked.

"Yes, I am," answered Philip.

The band leader looked surprised. "I expected to find the player much older," he said. "But it doesn't matter. It doesn't matter a bit." Then, looking up, he held out his hand and smiled. "I'm Jim Russell," he said.

"And I'm John Philip Sousa," said Philip.

Mr. Russell took off his big hat and held it in his hand. "I'd like to talk with you for a few minutes," he said. "May I come in?"

"Of course," answered Philip, motioning for the band leader to come inside. "We can talk in our living room," he said. "My brothers and sisters are outside, so we'll not be disturbed."

Philip started to put his violin into its case, but Mr. Russell stopped him. "No, no," he said. "Don't put it away. I'd like to hear you play some more. Please play another piece."

The band leader looked at Philip. He still couldn't believe that Philip was so young. Finally he asked, "How old are you, anyhow?"

"Thirteen," Philip replied.

"Just thirteen?" Mr. Russell now seemed to be thinking of something far away. "Have you ever thought of joining the circus?"

"Joining the circus!" Philip exclaimed. He thought that he hadn't heard correctly. "I—I don't know what you mean."

"Well, I'll explain," said Mr. Russell. "I need musicians for my band. When I was passing the house, I heard you playing. Then I stopped to listen and decided to talk with you."

Mr. Russell looked at Philip again. "Of course, you're very young," he said, "much younger than the other members of the band. But, after all, it isn't age that counts. People listen to music to enjoy it—not to check up on the ages of the players. Do you play any other instruments besides the violin?"

"Oh, yes," replied Philip. "I play the cymbals, the alto horn and——"

"Alto horn!" exclaimed Mr. Russell, very much pleased. "How would you like to join the band and play the alto horn for us? You'll get your room and board and a salary——"

Philip didn't answer. He just sat thinking in a sort of dream. He thought of how wonderful it would be to march along streets and play in the parade. He thought of how wonderful it would be to play inside the circus tent.

He'd have a chance to meet all the circus people and watch them work. He would travel and visit many places that he had never dreamed of seeing. And he'd be paid for traveling. Philip smiled. He felt as if someone had offered to pay him for eating a special birthday dinner.

Mr. Russell waited patiently. He could imagine what Philip was thinking, because he knew that every boy dreamed of joining a circus. Somehow he felt that sooner or later Philip would say yes.

But Philip now began to think of the other side of things. He began to think of his father and mother. He knew that they wouldn't be pleased about his joining a circus.

At last Philip started to talk. "I'd love to join the circus, Mr. Russell. I'd love to march in the parade and play in the circus band. But I'm sure that my father and mother won't let me take a job with a circus."

Mr. Russell seemed greatly disappointed in Philip's answer. He hadn't expected Philip to refuse. He needed a horn player. He must think of another way of persuading Philip to accept.

For a few moments he just leaned back in his chair and closed his eyes. Then he sat up quickly and exclaimed, "I have an idea. Don't tell your parents. Just come with us when we leave tomorrow. After a day or two you can write them a letter to let them know where you are. You can tell them that you have a good job.

"If you ask them now," he went on, "they probably will say no. They won't understand what a great chance you have. But after you're gone—after they know you're all right—they'll be just as happy as you are."

Philip shook his head. "I'd never leave without telling them," he said. "Why, they'd worry themselves sick if I'd leave home. They'd think that something had happened to me."

Mr. Russell rubbed his forehead. Somehow he must get Philip to say yes.

At that moment the younger Sousa children came into the house. They raced through the hall, shouting to one another.

Mr. Russell looked at Philip. "Are those children your brothers and sisters?" he asked.

Philip nodded.

"Are there many children in your family?"

"There are eight of us."

"Eight! My, that's a large family for your

148

father and mother to take care of. Don't you think that a boy of your age should be earning his own living? Surely you don't want to stay at home and be a burden to your parents."

A burden? Philip felt puzzled. He had never thought of himself as a burden to his parents. His father and mother had always seemed to be proud of their large family. He knew that they weren't rich, but they always seemed to have enough money for things that were needed. They even had enough money for him to take music lessons.

Perhaps he was a burden. Only that morning his father had told his mother that she worked too hard. If he went with the circus, there would be one less person for her to cook for. And his salary—he could send part of that home.

Suddenly Philip was sure that he ought to take the job. "All right," he said. "I'll go with you. I'll be at the circus grounds tomorrow."

"Good! Good!" Mr. Russell felt very pleased with himself. Then, looking at the clock, he jumped to his feet. "I didn't know it was so late," he said. "If I don't hurry, I'll miss the afternoon performance."

Mr. Russell handed Philip a card. "Here, take this," he said, "and show it to the manager to-morrow afternoon. I'll tell him that you're coming."

All at once Philip had something to ask Mr. Russell. "Will the circus come back to Washington next year?"

"I'm sure that it will," replied Mr. Russell. "Washington is one of the best cities in the country. We never miss coming here."

"If the circus comes back," Philip went on, "may I have free tickets for my family? May I have nine free tickets?"

"Of course." Now Mr. Russell was ready to promise anything. "You may count on nine free tickets. Well," he said, hurrying on, "I'll see you when we strike the tents tomorrow."

"Strike the tents?" Philip looked puzzled. "What does that mean?"

"When a circus breaks up and moves on to another city we call it 'striking the tents.'" Mr. Russell looked at Philip and went on talking. "You'll meet new people. You'll see new towns. And," he called back over his shoulder, "you'll learn a new language—circus language."

"That's what I'm doing," said Philip to himself as he turned back into the house. "I'm leaving. I'm moving on to another town. I'm going to strike the tents, too."

Philip closed the door and walked into the living room. He put his violin back into its case. It was hard for him to believe that he was about to join a circus. A few minutes before, he had been only a thirteen-year-old boy, trying to play a circus tune. Now he had a job in a circus band.

"Lucky me," said Philip, thinking about when he would come back next year. "Just wait until a year from now. I'll come back with front-row tickets for Mamma and Papa and all the children. And they'll see me playing in the circus band. They'll really be proud of me." He took a deep breath at the thought. He was sure that he never had been so happy.

Again he began to think about leaving his family and friends. Then he found that he was not happy, but unhappy.

He shook his head. How could he be so happy and unhappy all at the same time?

At this, he threw back his head and squared his shoulders. "Well," he said, "if I'm going to strike the tents tomorrow, I should start packing." A strange sound came from his throat. He couldn't tell whether it was a laugh or a sob. He rushed outdoors. He didn't want to be alone.

The Carpetbag

PHILIP stood in his yard and looked toward the Accardi house next door. Edward Accardi and Philip had been friends for a long time.

Philip knew that he would miss Edward as much as he would his own family. And he knew that Edward would miss him, too. Suddenly he felt he should tell Edward his secret. He couldn't keep it to himself any longer.

Philip ran across the lawn and jumped over the low fence that divided the two yards.

"Ed! Hey, Ed."

"What do you want?" Edward looked out of an upstairs window.

"I have something to tell you."

Edward crawled out the window, climbed along a limb, and slid down the trunk of a tree. He saluted Philip and clicked his heels together. "Here I am, Mr. Sousa. At your service."

This was Edward's usual way of leaving his bedroom to talk with Philip.

"Ahem!" Philip cleared his throat. "What do you mean, reporting for inspection with a black smudge on your chin?"

Edward rubbed his face. "I got the smudge while reporting for duty, sir," he said. "A tree got in my way."

"Well!" Philip looked very stern. "If you're going to run into trees, what will happen when you meet the enemy?"

"I'll run into them, too, sir." With this, Edward saluted again.

Philip returned the salute. "For that, I'll let you help me escape," he said.

154

"Escape?" Edward pretended to reach for a gun. "You're not running away, are you, sir?"

Philip sat down on the grass and pulled Edward down beside him. "Listen, Ed, I have something important to tell you."

"I'm all ears," said Edward, sitting down and leaning against the trunk of a tree. "Go on and tell me what you wish to say."

Philip looked down at his friend. The two of them were always pretending things. They were always making up wild tales to see which one could outdo the other. Now Philip realized that he would have a hard time making Edward believe him. He even would have a hard time believing himself.

"Ed."

"Yes?"

"What I'm going to tell you is really true. Honest-to-goodness, it is."

"Sure, I know." Edward wondered what kind

155

of wild story Philip was going to tell him this time, but he didn't care. Already he had thought of a story of his own that he felt would be better than any story Philip might tell him.

"Ed."

"Yes?"

"Ed, look at me."

Edward did as Philip asked. Something in Philip's voice sounded strange.

"Ed." Philip put his hand on Edward's sleeve. "Ed, what I'm going to tell you is true. Cross my heart and hope to die."

Edward blinked his eyes. "All right, Philip," he said. "I believe you."

"Do you cross your heart and hope to die?"

"I cross my heart and hope to die."

"All right. Now that you really believe me, I'll tell you." Philip took Mr. Russell's card out of his pocket and showed it to Edward. Then, in a few minutes, he told him the whole story.

156

"Whew!" Edward gave a low whistle. "Well, you certainly are lucky, but how am I going to get along without you? I'll be lonesome, more lonesome than I can tell you."

"Lonesome?" Philip jumped up. *Lonesome* was a word he was trying to forget. "Listen," he said, "I have to pack. Do you want to help me?"

"Sure," Edward nodded.

Philip walked slowly back and forth. "I've been thinking," he said. "How am I going to get my things out of the house without being seen? My brothers and sisters run all over the house."

"H-m-m-m." Edward chewed on a piece of grass thoughtfully. Then he had an idea. "I know," he said, "get an empty carpetbag and take it to your bedroom.

"When no one is around, throw the carpetbag down to me and I'll hide it under my bed," he went on. "Then bring your things over to my house to pack them."

"Well—" Philip looked a little uncertain— "how can we get the carpetbag out of your house tomorrow without being caught?"

"Oh, that will be easy." Edward grinned. "Mamma is going to the grocery tomorrow, and we can take the bag out while she's away. You see, it's sometimes very nice to be the only child in a family."

A few minutes later the boys went to the Sousa attic to look for a carpetbag.

"Here's one." Philip brushed off a few cobwebs with his hand. "It's an old one. I don't think Mamma will mind if I use it."

Edward nodded. "Take it down to your bedroom," he said, "while I go outside. If there's no one around, I'll whistle to you. Then you can throw it down to me from your window."

Edward ran downstairs, through the house and out into the yard. He looked up and down the street. He looked at the windows in the

Sousa house. He looked at the windows in his own house. There was no one in sight.

Now that everything seemed safe, Edward whistled to Philip. "All right, Philip," he called. "Throw down the carpetbag."

Edward held out his arms, and Philip threw down the bag. The heavy bag hit Edward on the chest and knocked him down. Philip ran downstairs and outside as fast as he could go. "Are you all right?" he asked.

Edward looked up and started to grin. "You got down almost as fast as the bag," he said, getting up from the ground. "Of course I'm all right. The bag just knocked the wind out of me for a minute. And the bag's all right, too, but we must hurry. We must get the bag into the house before someone sees us."

Philip carried many things over to Edward's house that afternoon. He piled everything on the bed in Edward's room.

"Look, we'll never get all these things in that carpetbag," said Edward. The bed was loaded with clothes and all sorts of things.

"Of course we will." Philip began to fold his suit. He folded his trousers readily, but didn't know how to fold his coat. "Say," he said to Edward, "how do you fold a coat?"

"I don't know."

The two boys put the coat on the floor and tried to fold it first one way and then another, but the sleeves always got in the way. They tried to fold some shirts, but those sleeves got in the way, too. "You, know," said Edward after a few minutes, "these surely are circus clothes, all right."

"Circus clothes?" repeated Philip. "What do you mean by that?"

"Why, your coat and shirts seem to have a dozen sleeves," said Edward. "I never saw anything with so many sleeves."

Finally the boys finished packing the bag. Edward held it together while Philip fastened it. Just then the boys heard the back door close. Someone had come.

"That's Mamma," Edward whispered. "Hurry! Push the bag under my bed. It will be safe there until tomorrow."

That evening Philip was too excited to eat much supper. He was too excited to go to bed, but he had to go anyhow. He was sure, however, that he wouldn't sleep.

"I wonder where I'll be tomorrow night," he said to himself as he climbed into bed. "I wonder what city I'll be in, and where I'll be sleeping. I wonder—" Philip closed his eyes— "I wonder what the city will be like—I wonder—I wonder——"

Philip was sound asleep.

The Sunday Suit

When Philip opened his eyes the next morning, Mr. Sousa was standing beside his bed. "Good morning, Philip," he said. "It's time for you to get up. And when you dress," he added, "be sure to put on your Sunday clothes."

Mr. Sousa hurried from the room. He didn't say anything more—not a word.

Philip sat up in bed. What did his father mean? Why did he want him to put on his Sunday clothes? What could be going on?

Then Philip remembered that his Sunday suit was at Edward's house in the carpetbag.

"What shall I do? What——" Philip started

163

to get up. As he turned, he noticed his Sunday
suit hanging over a chair beside the bed.

Philip rubbed his eyes. There must be some
mistake! He had packed his suit in the carpetbag and put it under Edward's bed.

He jumped up and ran to the chair. He looked
at the suit carefully and tried on the coat.

He sat down on the chair to think. Had he
been having a silly dream?

A band leader wearing a bright red and white uniform wouldn't stop at the Sousa house. He wouldn't offer a thirteen-year-old boy a job to play in a circus band. Mr. Russell wasn't real. He was just part of a dream.

Next Philip thought about packing the carpet-bag in Edward's room. His coat and shirts seemed to have had a dozen sleeves.

Philip shook his head. Everything that he remembered from the day before seemed very strange. Not a thing seemed true.

Then Philip shook his head again. There had been no dream. Mr. Russell was real. The things he and Edward had done—they were real, too.

There still was a question about his suit. Who had taken it out of the bag and brought it to his room in the middle of the night?

Philip was too puzzled to straighten things out in his mind. Finally he decided to finish dressing and go downstairs.

By now it was fairly late. All the other members of the family had finished breakfast. No one was in the dining room.

Philip felt strange eating alone at the big table. "I feel so puzzled about everything this morning," he said to himself. "Being puzzled is like reading an exciting book. You can hardly wait to turn the next page to see what's going to happen."

When he was through, Philip went to the living room. "Ah!" Mr. Sousa looked up from his paper. "I see you are ready. We'd better start."

Again something strange was happening. Philip was becoming more puzzled all the time. He didn't know what his father was talking about, or where they were going.

Mr. Sousa and Philip walked briskly down the street. They kept walking until they came to the Marine Barracks. They walked through the gate, across the Parade Grounds and into an office

building. Then they climbed some steps that led to General Zeilin's office on the second floor.

General Zeilin was the Commandant of the Marine Corps. Philip had heard his father speak of him, but he had never met him before.

"Good morning, Philip." General Zeilin was very friendly.

"Good morning, sir." Philip looked first at the Commandant and then at his father. He couldn't imagine why he was here.

General Zeilin stood up and held out his hand. "Welcome to the Marines, Philip," he said. "I have placed you in the Marine Band. I'm sure that you'll be a valuable member."

Philip was too surprised to say anything. He stared at his father and General Zeilin.

Mr. Sousa smiled. "This is a big surprise for Philip," he explained. "I didn't tell him anything about coming here."

He looked at Philip. "I hope you're pleased,

Philip," he said. 'Your mother and I have talked about your joining the Marines. And I have talked with General Zeilin about your joining. He says that he will be glad to have you, but you don't have to join, if you don't want to."

Philip took a deep breath. Was he still dreaming? Yesterday he had been asked to join the circus. Today he had a chance to join the Marines. "Well," he thought, "if I'm dreaming, I like today's dream better than yesterday's."

"Thank you, sir," said Philip, standing up very straight. He smiled at General Zeilin. "I'll be proud and happy to be a member of the United States Marines."

General Zeilin opened his desk drawer and took out a printed form. On the top line he wrote the date: June 9, 1868. On the second line he wrote: John Philip Sousa. Then he paused and looked at Philip. "When were you born?" he asked.

"November 6, 1854," Philip answered.

"Let's see." General Zeilin did a little figuring. "That makes you thirteen-and-a-half years old. Is that right?"

"Yes, sir."

General Zeilin smiled. "Well, you're a little young to join the Marines, but we can use you in the band. You'll start as an apprentice musician. This means that you'll study under some regular player. But you'll really be in the Marines," General Zeilin went on. "You won't be able to leave without getting permission."

"I understand, sir," said Philip, standing up even straighter than before. "I'll do my very best to be a good marine, sir."

"I'm sure that you will." General Zeilin finished filling out the form and handed it to Philip. "You are to report for duty tomorrow morning."

Then General Zeilin stood up and shook hands with Philip. "Good luck," he said.

170

Philip and his father started home. At first Philip didn't say anything. He was still too puzzled to talk. By and by he thought of a dozen questions to ask.

"Papa?"

"Yes?"

"I——" Philip didn't know which one of his questions to ask first.

Mr. Sousa threw back his head and laughed. "All right, Philip," he said. "I know you're puzzled, so I'll explain everything.

"Thank the rain," Mr. Sousa began. "Yes, thank the rain for everything."

"The rain?" Philip felt more puzzled than ever. What did his father mean?

"You know," Mr. Sousa went on, "that we had a hard rain last night. The rain came up very suddenly. Did you hear it?"

Philip shook his head. He had been too sound asleep to hear anything.

Mr. Sousa looked at Philip a moment before he went on. "There was a strong wind with the rain. The wind blew the rain through Edward's window. Mrs. Accardi went to close the window and found water on the floor. She had to move Edward's bed to wipe the floor."

Mr. Sousa looked at Philip out of the corner of his eye. Then, clearing his throat, he continued. "When Mrs. Accardi moved the bed, she saw a strange carpetbag on the floor. At first she thought that it belonged to Edward—that he had found it somewhere. Then she opened it and found that the things inside were yours.

"Mrs. Accardi didn't know what to do about the bag. Finally she decided to bring it over to our house and tell us about it.

"Your mother and I couldn't imagine what you were planning to do. Before long we found Mr. Russell's card. Then we were sure that you were planning to leave with the circus."

"Oh, Papa!" At first Philip didn't know what to say. But in a few minutes he managed to tell everything that had happened.

When he had finished, Mr. Sousa nodded. "I understand, son," he said. "Almost every boy like you wants to join a circus some time in his life. But Mamma and I, we couldn't get along without you. Neither could Edward. Mr. Russell was wrong to make you think that you should leave home."

Mr. Sousa smiled. "Now I'll tell you the rest of my story," he said. "Mamma and I know that once a boy decides to get a job, it's pretty hard to stop him. So we made up our minds to help you find work right here in Washington." Mr. Sousa patted Philip's shoulder. "You see, we want you as near us as possible.

"Then I happened to think of General Zeilin," Mr. Sousa went on. "He's a good friend of mine, and he has several boys of his own. I knew that he'd understand. Anyhow, he had told me that he needed musicians for the Marine Band."

As Philip and his father walked on, it began to rain. "Ah!" Mr. Sousa threw back his head to let the rain fall on his face. "Rain is nice. It cools the air. It makes things grow. Sometimes it even keeps boys in Washington."

Philip lifted his face, too. "Yes, rain is wonderful," he said. "Sometimes it even gets a boy into the United States Marines."

Suddenly Philip remembered that yesterday he had been both happy and unhappy at the same time. Now he was only happy, because he had no reason to be unhappy. It was much nicer this way.

The Big Opportunity

PHILIP had been with the Marine Band for six months. One day Mr. Scala, the band leader, had a special talk with him.

"I've been watching you, Philip," he said. "You're a fine musician. Your father tells me you practice a great deal on your violin when you're at home. He says you would like to do some composing, too."

"Yes, sir." Philip looked embarrassed. "I would like to compose. I'm taking lessons from Mr. Felix Benkert now. He is a fine teacher. And I play first violin in his Orchestral Union. But I still have much to learn."

Mr. Scala nodded. "I know that studying music isn't easy," he said, "that's why I want to talk with you. I think it would be a good idea for you to go to Europe to study music."

"Europe?" asked Philip. "That sounds wonderful, sir, but how would I get there? My parents can't afford to send me and—" Philip looked at the band leader and smiled— "well, you know, sir, I get only thirteen dollars a month as a private in the Marines. I never could save enough to pay my own way."

"I know," Mr. Scala said, "but I have another plan. There's a man here in Washington who is very wealthy, Mr. W. W. Corcoran. He's interested in young musicians and is often willing to help them. Perhaps if you talked with him, he would send you to Europe."

Philip shook his head. "I don't think I'd like that. I wouldn't want a stranger to support me. I'd feel as if I owed him too much."

176

"You don't understand," Mr. Scala went on. "Mr. Corcoran likes to help young people. He has plenty of money. Why shouldn't you let him help you, if he wants to do it?"

Mr. Scala shook Philip's shoulder gently. "Come on," he said. "Don't be so stubborn. Let me talk with him. Then if he's interested, you can go to see him later."

"Well, all right," agreed Philip. But he didn't sound convinced.

A few days later Mr. Scala stopped Philip again. "I talked with Mr. Corcoran," he said. "He'd like to see you. I told him that you would come to his house tomorrow afternoon."

Mr. Scala gave Philip a card with the address on it. "Be sure to start early," he said. "Mr. Corcoran lives a long way from your home."

At one o'clock the next afternoon, Philip left home. When the horse-drawn streetcar stopped at the corner, he jumped on and paid his fare.

Before long, he was in a part of Washington where he never had been before.

Philip watched for street signs. When he reached the proper corner, he got off and started to walk. As he went along, he looked at the big houses along the street. He had never known there were so many large houses in Washington. Most of them were built in the center of whole city blocks. Often Philip couldn't even see the houses from the sidewalk.

Finally Philip found the right street and the right number. "Whew!" He stopped and stared. Mr. Corcoran's house seemed even larger than the others he had passed. It looked more like a public building than a private home.

Philip walked along a stone wall until he came to some iron gates, which were partly open. Trees lined the long walk that led to the house. The entrance to the house had iron gates, too, but these were closed.

178

Philip pulled at the bell timidly. He was afraid that he wouldn't know how to act here. He was sorry that he had come.

Philip waited for what seemed a long time. "Maybe the bell didn't ring," he said to himself. "Maybe Mr. Corcoran forgot I was coming. Maybe there's no one at home."

Philip smiled. There had to be someone at home in a big house like this. There had to be a servant or a caretaker or——

The big gates opened and a footman appeared. He was wearing a blue uniform with a cutaway coat and knee breeches.

"Yes?" He didn't look at Philip. Instead, he stared straight ahead.

The footman made Philip feel like a beggar. Philip wanted to turn around and run away. But he knew that he couldn't leave now. What would Mr. Scala say if he did?

Philip stood up straight. He wasn't going to

let the footman frighten him. "I have an appointment with Mr. Corcoran," he said, trying to sound important. "He's expecting me."

The footman made a stiff right-hand turn. Philip wanted to laugh. "We do an about-face better in the Marines," he thought.

Philip followed the footman down a long hallway. Large pictures hung on the walls. Beautiful carpet covered the floor. Silk draperies hung at the windows.

The footman led Philip into a room. "Wait here," he said and motioned for Philip to sit down. Then he left the room.

A few minutes later Mr. Corcoran appeared. He was kind and friendly. He asked Philip a great many questions.

After they had talked for some time, Mr. Corcoran said, "I've talked to a number of people about you. All of them say that you are a fine musician. But I have many people coming to

180

me for help. Let me think about your case for a while. Come to see me again in a few days."

Philip hurried down the long walk toward the street. Mr. Corcoran had seemed interested. He had been kind and friendly. But Philip was glad to get out of the big house. He had been uncomfortable all the time he was there.

"If Mr. Corcoran sends me to Europe," Philip thought, "I'll be responsible to him for everything I do. He'll have a right to tell me where to go and where to stay. He'll have a right to choose my teachers."

Suddenly Philip knew that he had to be free to follow his own ideas. A whole world of music stretched before him. He wanted to play an instrument. He wanted to direct a band. He wanted to compose music. But he had to do these things by himself, in his own way.

All at once Philip knew that having Mr. Corcoran send him to Europe wasn't his "big opportunity" after all. His "big opportunity" was within himself.

Philip threw back his head and laughed. He felt wonderfully free and happy. A new melody formed itself in his head. A new melody—— Philip looked down at his feet. He wasn't walking any longer. He was marching now. He was keeping time to that little tune inside his head. It seemed to say, "Hurry, hurry. Step lively now. You have a long, long way to go."

Philip stopped beside the gates in the stone wall. "When I go to Europe," he said in a loud, firm voice— "when I go to Europe, I'll go on my own. No one is going to send me."

The March King

MANY years later John Philip Sousa and his wife paced the deck of an ocean liner. They were returning from a vacation in Europe. It was a cold stormy day in November, 1896.

Faster and faster Mr. Sousa walked, with the wind whistling about his ears. All the while he kept his eyes on the American flag, floating proudly above him. The brisk wind kept the flag flying straight and stiff. He could see every star and every stripe. He forgot all about Mrs. Sousa, who was trying to keep up with him.

"Not so fast, Philip," said Mrs. Sousa. "I can't keep up with you."

Mr. Sousa stopped at once. "I'm sorry," he said. "I was thinking——"

"I know. You were thinking of another march!" his wife laughed. "Will you never run out of ideas? I've lost track of how many marches you have composed now."

Mr. and Mrs. Sousa leaned on the ship's rail and looked at the green water all about them. As John Philip Sousa looked, he seemed to hear beautiful music coming up from the waves.

Once more he looked at the stars and stripes above him. He imagined that they were keeping time as they fluttered in the wind.

Mrs. Sousa did not interrupt her husband's thoughts. She knew what that look in his eyes meant. He seemed to be listening to something that she could not hear.

The sound seemed to swell around him. He heard hundreds of feet marching. The flag above waved in perfect time to the rhythm. It seemed to beckon to him.

John Philip Sousa fell into step with the music. He seemed to hear a chorus of voices.

After that, whenever Mr. Sousa came on deck, the same melody filled his ears. When he reached New York, every note of the tune was as clear to him as though he had heard it played.

The three Sousa children were happy to see their parents again. They enjoyed all the little gifts that their parents had brought them from

Europe. They enjoyed hearing their parents tell about the places they had visited.

At last Mr. Sousa excused himself. He went to his study and closed the door. He sat down at his desk and quickly put on paper the music for "The Stars and Stripes Forever."

When he had finished, he went back to the living room, waving the papers over his head. "This is the best one yet," he said. " 'The Stars and Stripes Forever.' Wait until you hear it."

Helen said, "Oh, Papa, you say that about every march you write. I know it can't be as good as 'Semper Fidelis.' "

John Philip, Jr. said, "It can't be better than 'The Washington Post.' "

"Now, children," said Mrs. Sousa. "Each of your father's compositions has its own place. All of them are special. They bring brightness and happiness to everyone. I am sure that 'The Stars and Stripes Forever' will, too."

"Just the same," said Priscilla, "my favorite will always be 'The High School Cadets.' "

Mr. Sousa smiled as he sat down. "Mamma is right," he said. "Each one is special. I am lucky that I can make my living doing what I want to do more than anything else. It hasn't always been easy. But Mamma has never complained, even when we had very little money."

Mrs. Sousa looked up quickly. "I have never complained about you, no. Only the ones who took advantage of you have I complained about. Years ago, some people paid you only thirty-five dollars apiece for your marches!"

"I know, Mamma," Mr. Sousa nodded. "But that was before I became known as a composer. This march will be different."

Sure enough, John Philip Sousa was right about "The Stars and Stripes Forever." During his lifetime he collected a small fortune from the sheet music that was sold.

188

John Philip Sousa and his band toured all parts of the United States. They gave concerts from east to west and north to south. They made four concert tours of Europe, and one tour of the world. Mr. Sousa's programs always included the compositions of other composers. For encores he played some of his own compositions.

Whatever else John Philip Sousa played, one selection was always the same. Every audience demanded "The Stars and Stripes Forever."

With all his tours and his composing, John Philip Sousa found time for other things. He never was too busy to judge a contest for young musicians. He selected the winners, but secretly he always felt sorry for the losers. He hated to think how disappointed they must be.

John Philip Sousa lived to be seventy-seven years old. Only a few months before his death, he was one of the judges in a contest for young violin students. Each of the contestants had already won at least one contest. This was the final one.

The proud parents and friends of the students filled the hall. Many other persons came because they wanted to see John Philip Sousa. The second judge was another well-known musician, and the third was a music teacher.

A local band played while the crowd gathered. When Mr. Sousa entered the hall, the band swung into "The Stars and Stripes Forever." The audience rose to its feet as if someone had pushed a button. Mr. Sousa smiled and bowed as he took his place with the other two judges.

One after another, the student violinists came out on the stage and played. Mr. Sousa listened intently. Perhaps he was thinking of the long hard hours he had spent practicing.

As each contestant played, each judge wrote down a score. The highest score was 100. At the end of the contest, the judges took their

folded slips of paper and went into another room. The lady who was to announce the winner went into the room with them.

When the lady unfolded the slips of paper with the scores on them, she and the other two judges were amazed. On each slip, Mr. Sousa had carefully written the same score—100.

Mr. Sousa threw back his head and laughed when he saw how surprised the others were. "Forgive an old man his little joke," he said. "All of the students tried so hard. I couldn't bear to discourage a single one of them."

The other two judges had, without knowing it, agreed on the same contestant as the winner. So the results would have been the same, even if Mr. Sousa had chosen a different winner.

The audience clapped and cheered when the winner was announced. After the hall was quiet again, the announcer said, "All the contestants have won today, even the losers. They have won because they have had a chance to play for John Philip Sousa, 'The March King.'"

More About This Book

WHEN JOHN PHILIP SOUSA LIVED

1854   JOHN PHILIP SOUSA WAS BORN IN WASHINGTON, D.C., NOVEMBER 6.

There were thirty-one states in the Union.

Franklin D. Pierce was President.

The population of the country was about 26,670,000.

1854–   PHILIP LIVED WITH HIS PARENTS AND STARTED
1867   TO STUDY MUSIC AT THE AGE OF FIVE.

Harriet Beecher Stowe's *Uncle Tom's Cabin* was published, 1852.

The Lincoln-Douglas debates were held in Illinois, 1858.

The War between the States was fought, 1861-1865.

President Abraham Lincoln issued the Emancipation Proclamation, 1863.

The first Pullman railroad sleeping car was built, 1864.

The United States purchased Alaska, 1867.

**YOUNG SOUSA JOINED THE MARINE BAND AND
LATER DIRECTED AN ORCHESTRA.**

The first transcontinental railroad was completed, 1869.

Alexander G. Bell invented the telephone, 1876.

Bicycles were first made in America, 1878.

Thomas Edison invented the phonograph, 1878, and the electric light bulb, 1879.

1880– **SOUSA SERVED AS LEADER OF THE MARINE
1892 BAND AND BEGAN TO COMPOSE MUSIC.**

James A. Garfield became President and was assassinated, 1881.

Clara Barton founded the American Red Cross, 1881.

Thomas Edison invented the motion picture camera, 1889.

1892– **SOUSA ORGANIZED HIS OWN BAND, TRAVELED
1932 WIDELY, AND CONTINUED TO COMPOSE MUSIC.**

Henry Ford built his first automobile, 1893.

The Spanish-American War was fought, 1898.

Wilbur and Orville Wright flew their first airplane, 1903.

The First World War was fought, 1914-1918.

194

1932   JOHN PHILIP SOUSA DIED, MARCH 6.

Herbert Hoover was President.

There were forty-eight states in the Union.

The population of the country was about
124,370,000.

DO YOU REMEMBER?

1. Where did the Sousa family live when Philip was
a boy?

2. How did Philip get to take singing lessons when
he was only five years of age?

3. What unusual instrument did Mr. Sousa take out
of the chest to show Philip?

4. How did the children find and return Mr. Esputa's
lost spectacles?

5. What kind of instruction did Philip take at John
Esputa's music school?

6. What happened when Philip thought that he
wanted to become a baker?

7. How did Philip get to play with the Marine Band
on the White House lawn?

8. Why did Philip and his father join the parade
following the War between the States?

9. How did Philip come to compose a new melody after attending a concert?

10. What kept Philip from joining the circus band passing through Washington?

11. How did Philip get an opportunity to join the Marine Band in Washington?

12. Why did Philip decide that he didn't want to go to Europe to study music?

13. How did John Philip Sousa come to compose "The Stars and Stripes Forever"?

14. What kind of concerts did Sousa give on his tours of America and Europe?

15. What popular title did he acquire?

IT'S FUN TO LOOK UP THESE THINGS

1. What is the United States Marine Band, which is referred to in the story?

2. How do the instruments in a band differ from the instruments in an orchestra?

3. What is vocal music and how does it differ from instrumental music?

4. Why are marches usually played by bands rather than by orchestras?

196

5. How many years did Sousa take his famous band on tours in this country and abroad?

6. What are the names of some of Sousa's popular marches besides "The Stars and Stripes Forever"?

7. What other American composers of music are noted chiefly for their marches?

INTERESTING THINGS YOU CAN DO

1. Look for a photograph of Sousa's band to place on the bulletin board.

2. Listen to a recording of Sousa's famous march, "The Stars and Stripes Forever."

3. Tap with a pencil to keep time with music selections you hear on radio and television.

4. Find out what a bandmaster does in training and directing a band.

5. Make a list of music selections which you recognize when you hear them.

6. Describe some of the most important instruments played in a band.

7. Name a few band leaders who are popular in our country today.

OTHER BOOKS YOU MAY ENJOY READING

Bands Play On: The Story of Bands and Orchestras, The, Irmengarde Eberle (pseud. P. A. Carter). McBride.

From These Comes Music: Instruments of the Band and Orchestra, Hope Stoddard. Crowell.

Horn That Stopped the Band, The, Arthur Hudson Parsons. Watts.

John Philip Sousa, the March King, Mina Lewton Simon. Didier.

Little Brass Band, The, Margaret Wise Brown. Harper.

Story-Lives of American Composers, Katherine Bakeless. Lippincott.

INTERESTING WORDS IN THIS BOOK

acrobat (ăk′rṓ băt) : person who does stunts that require strength or skill

alto horn (ăl′tō) : horn sometimes used in place of a French horn

apprentice (ă prĕn′tĭs) : person learning a trade or profession

banister (băn′ĭs tẽr) : stair railing

198

barracks (băr'ăks) : buildings where military persons, except commissioned officers, live

baton (bă'tôn) : wand or slender, rounded wooden rod, which a person uses to direct the numbers of an orchestra or band

bunting (bŭn'tĭng) : cloth the color of flags used for decorations

cadet (kȧ dĕt') : young man taking military training

capital (kăp'ĭ tăl) : city where the government of a country or state is located

composer (kŏm pōz'ẽr) : person who writes music

confusion (kōn fū'zhŭn) : state of being mixed up

congratulate (kŏn grăt ū'lāt) : express pleasure at some sort of good fortune

courtyard (kōrt'yärd) : area enclosed by walls

cymbals (sĭm'bălz) : round brass plates, which make a ringing noise when struck together

emergency (ė mûr'jĕn sĭ) : something that demands immediate solution or action

harmony (här'mȯ nĭ) : combination of musical sounds that sound well together

instrument (ĭn'stro͝o mĕnt) : device for producing musical sounds, as a piano or violin

knead (nēd) : work over with the hands

Marine Corps (má rēn′ kōr) : branch of the Navy that fights on both land and sea

musician (mů zĭsh′ăn) : person skilled in music, a composer or professional performer

orchestra (ôr′kĕs trä) : group of musicians who play different instruments together

profession (prȯ fĕsh′ŭn) : work that requires special education

rhythm (rĭth'm) : movement with a regular beat or accent

ridiculous (rĭ dĭk′ů lŭs) : laughable

rosette (rȯ zĕt) : design that looks like a rose

scale: series of notes or musical sounds rising regularly in tone

Semper Fidelis (sĕm′pẽr fĭ dē′lĭs) : title of one of Sousa's most popular marches, Latin words meaning "always faithful"

tone: musical sound

triangle (trī′ăng′g'l) : musical instrument, shaped like a triangle, that gives a ringing sound when hit

trombone (trŏm′bōn) : long musical wind instrument with a section that slides back and forth

Childhood

OF FAMOUS AMERICANS

CHILDHOOD OF FAMOUS AMERICANS

COLONIAL DAYS

DOLLY MADISON, *Monsell*

JAMES OGLETH
JOHN ALDEN, *Bu*
JOHN PETER ZENG
JOHN SMITH, *Bart*
MYLES STANDISH,
PETER STUYVESAN
PHILLIS WHEATLE
  Speicher
POCAHONTAS, *Se*
PONTIAC, *Peckha*
SQUANTO, *Steven*
VIRGINIA DARE,
WILLIAM BRADFO
WILLIAM PENN, *N*

STRUGGLE
INDEPEND

ANTHONY WAYNI
BEN FRANKLIN, *S*
BETSY ROSS, *Wei*
CRISPUS ATTUCK
DAN MORGAN, *B*
ETHAN ALLEN, *W*
FRANCIS MARION
GEORGE ROGERS
GEORGE WASHIN
ISRAEL PUTNAM,
JOHN HANCOCK,
JOHN PAUL JONE
MARTHA WASHIN
MOLLY PITCHER,
NATHAN HALE, *S*
NATHANAEL GRE
PATRICK HENRY,
PAUL REVERE, *St*
TOM JEFFERSON,

EARLY NATIONAL
GROWTH

ABIGAIL ADAMS, *Wagoner*
ALEC HAMILTON, *Higgins*
ANDY JACKSON, *Stevenson*
BENJAMIN WEST, *Snow*
BLACK HAWK, *Cleven*
DAN WEBSTER, *Smith*
DEWITT CLINTON, *Widdemer*

MERIWETHER LEWIS, *Devenroth*
NARCISSA WHITMAN, *Warner*
SACAGAWEA, *Seymour*
SAM HOUSTON, *Stevenson*
SIMON KENTON, *Wilkie*
  Stevenson
WILL CLARK, *Wilkie*
WILLIAM FARGO, *Wilkie*
WILLIAM HENRY HARRISON, *Peckham*
ZEB PIKE, *Stevenson*